A Family in the F

The Grovers of Ealing

Eileen Sanderson

To

Marie

From.

Eileen.

X

ISBN 978-1-5262-0715-9

Dedication

To three people who I miss who brought fun, laughter and love to my life: my mum, Kathleen, my aunt Elizabeth and my sister Jo.

Contents

Acknowledgements

On a recent "decluttering" campaign in my home I re-discovered a dissertation I had written in 1991 for the Diploma in History of the Family and Genealogy at the Centre for Extra Mural Studies at Birkbeck College. Rather than put it back to the bottom of a drawer again I made the decision to revisit it again and put it together into this booklet.

Guidance and advice came for the initial dissertation from Michael Harris who was my tutor at Birkbeck College. The staff at the London Metropolitan Archives have been incredibly helpful. Jonathan Oates at Ealing Local History Library has shown great patience with my queries. Kath Shawcross and Mary Hartley have given me practical help. Help and encouragement has come from all quarters: my cousin Josie Reed kindly offered to retype the dissertation when I was faced with the first hurdle as my work was still on a floppy disc! I recently met Chris West from the London Historians, who will probably not even remember me, but he provided me with some positive comments and practical advice at a point where I was almost giving up on this project. I would also like to thank my brother Norrie Doyle who gave me advice and encouragement and finally I would like to thank my husband Kelvin who has consistently given me encouragement and moral support in all I do.

Abbreviations

L.M.A.	London Metropolitan Archives
T.N.A.	The National Archives

Chapter 1: The Undertaking Trade and Burial of the Poor 1650-1830

The growth and development of the Victorian funeral parlour, usually run by a family firm of undertakers, can be traced back to the epidemics of the seventeenth century which resulted in an unprecedented demand for individual coffins. (1) Previously, the coffin had been recycled by the local Parish Burial Guilds. (2) The body was placed in the coffin which was then transported to the grave on short poles carried at waist height and, after burial of the corpse, the coffin was washed down with vinegar and put away until the next time. The Parish Burial Society was responsible for the funeral arrangements of the members who had paid regular contributions. Later on Friendly Societies replaced them, but still retained the same aims and objectives. (3) Private enterprise was ready and able to fulfil the new demand for coffins, very often the same craftsmen who had worked for the Parish Burial Guilds. (4) The first known independent undertaker, William Russell, set himself up in London during the 1680s. (5) The specialist undertaker advertised his trade with the use of shop signs such as those shown in this booklet. (Illustration 1a, 1b, 1c)

An increasing movement towards private enterprise can be seen in a broadside dated c. 1720. (6) It contained an application made to the House of Commons from a group of men wishing to raise a Joint Stock Company "for the Undertaking and Furnishing of Funerals to any part of England". Private enterprise in the Undertaking trade was a risky business and to provide all the funerary services and trappings, including long distance funerals and the day to day village and town funerals was expensive and complicated. (7) Some still obtained business from contracting out work by the Friendly Societies in the 1760s. (8)

The unpredictable demand for funeral work is indicated by an inventory of Thomas Phill, an undertaker of St Martin's-in-the-Field dated 11th February 1717. (9) A large proportion of his stock was in pawn until it was required for a funeral. It included "thirteen old cloaks ten shillings more than pawned for". He also had "eight children's coffins of elm, four deal children's coffins, one six foot deal coffin, one work bench, some old tools with other timber". The number of children's coffins ready for use reflects the high infant mortality rate in this period.

By the mid eighteenth century private enterprise was firmly established in the undertaking trade and it was set for expansion. Many of the firms were family concerns and successful development was dependent upon the adoption of the trade by at least one member of each generation. Apprenticeship into the trade was known in some undertaking families and an apprenticeship indenture of 3rd July 1814 shows Joseph Taylor apprenticed to learn the "Art of an Undertaker" from Mark Anthony Low of Spitalfields for the sum of five pounds with the consent of the Churchwardens and Overseers of the Poor of the Parish of Hornsey. (10)

However, the funerals of the poor were not served by specialist undertakers. The compiler of a list of the undertakers using Wesley's Chapel, City Road for burials between 1799 and 1854 for burials noticed that:

Very often, the name of the undertaker is the same as that of the deceased, especially if a child. This suggests that no 'professional'

2

help was obtained in these cases, but that the parents brought the body to the grave themselves. A local carpenter would be asked to provide the coffin and for example Tooth, who was the builder of Wesley's Chapel was described as a builder and "not a specialist undertaker". (11)

The need to make arrangements for the burial of their own children can still be seen in the childhood recollections of one Lancashire woman who was asked by her mother to dispose of her still born baby, which was usually done by the midwife or parent. (12) The child lined a soap box with wadding and placed the "doll" in it, covered the box with black lining from her father's coat and took it with a letter to the grave digger. He told her to put "it" with the other "parcels" in the corner and that one such parcel was put in each public grave until they were nearly full up. (13)

The very idea of a pauper's burial was abhorrent to the poor. Burial on the parish invariably meant a plain coffin, no headstone and no funeral oration, although in some parishes it was known for the rates to provide ale for the mourners at the traditional "funeral feast". (14) Artists, such as Hogarth in his paintings "Gin Lane" and "The Harlot's Progress", depict the demise of the unfortunate prostitute or alcoholic and as Julian Litten comments they paint a tragic picture of the not-so-fortunates' last journey similar to one on a "a bare boarded coffin carried on the shoulders of four gin-mashers, the whole draped by a mean and insignificant pall". (15)

Rudimentary safeguards were used by the poor to protect graves from the body snatchers operating in mainly urban areas, such as London, particularly during the period 1750's to 1832. Watching the grave by members of the family or friends was sometimes resorted to, as was the mixing of sticks and straw with the earth of the grave –

to make it more difficult for the body snatchers' wooden shovel to dig the soil. (16) The development of the undertaking trade was given impetus by the purchase of elaborate triple coffins. These newly patented caskets were designed to offer further protection for the corpse. Burials in vaults provided extra protection from the body snatchers, though only for those who could afford this added expenditure.

By the 1830's the problem created by the burial of the dead in overcrowded churchyards, especially in London could no longer be ignored. Horrific stories of the use of quicklime to hasten the decomposition of the corpse, the theft of teeth, bones, coffin lead and timber were rife. (17) Instances such as the death of a grave digger and his would-be rescuer who, in the 1830s tumbled into a burial pit at St Botolph's, Aldgate, were frequently reported in the newspapers. (18) In this case, both victims probably died from the methane gases emitted from the corpses in the twenty foot deep hole. To address these problems Kensal Green cemetery was founded by a joint stock company in 1832 and from the 1830s other cemeteries were also established by joint stock companies and formed a cordon of seven cemeteries around London. (19) This ring of seven cemeteries consisted of Highgate Cemetery founded in 1839, Kensal Green (1832), Norwood, (1837), Nunhead (1840), Abney Park (1840), Brompton (1832) and Tower Hamlets (1841). As a result of the 1852 Burial Act which empowered London vestries to organise burial boards and provide new burial grounds of their own, a growing number of public cemeteries were founded. In the following chapters the funeral work and other services of one particular family, the Grover family of Ealing are examined in detail.

Chapter 2: The Funeral Business as a Family Tradition

Villages on the outskirts of London, such as Ealing, were home to the middle classes and the gentry and saw the establishment and growth of the undertaking trade. During the period looked at here, Ealing life was still centred in the area of the Parish Church of St Mary's, which had been rebuilt in 1733 after the tower had fallen down. A large yard, situated at Wisteria Cottage, close to the parish church of St Mary's Ealing, was the focal point for the Grover family undertakers of Ealing.

The first known information regarding the family was the marriage of James Grover to Hannah Timberlake on the 30th December 1771 a member of a local family. (1) They had nine children, including James and William who carried on the family craft of carpentry, building, joinery and undertaking. Their family history is charted in Table 1. According to an advertisement in the local newspaper, the Grover business was established by 1792 and by 1826 / 1827 the firm was listed in Pigot's Directory. In 1845 James Grover, the son of James and Hannah, died and his wife, Frances was left with seven children to bring up alone. One son, Francis, learnt the funeral business and joined the family firm after first considering becoming a grocer.

The first known ledger of business transactions compiled by the Grover firm survives from 1847. It is an organised and professionally kept record and comes from a period in the family business history when Frances Grover, the widow of James Grover (1785-1845), was nominally in charge of the firm. It was then a partnership with John Grover, the son of William (1790-1816), who had been taught the trade of joiner by his Uncle James. In 1847 John's wife, Grace, died and several years later he married Margaret, the widow of James Giles, the landlord of the nearby public house the New Inn. This inn must have been used frequently by the men working at the Grover's firm. John's sister Henrietta (bn. 1815) married a Peter Duffield and one of their sons, Henry Duffield also founded a building and undertaking business. It was situated in West Ealing and this family firm was still in operation in 1982.

John Grover died in 1877 and his partner Francis Grover carried on the business until his death in 1882 when his widow Eliza Martha ran it assisted by her sons. The photograph (Illustration on front cover) apparently shows her with her sons and daughters – Frank Charles Grover (bn. 1862), William Grover (bn. 1868), Jessica (bn. 1860) and Ada Florence (bn. 1865). Other members of the family also involved in the undertaking business lived locally at 1 Thorn Place (Illustration 2).

A local newspaper of 14th May 1892 carried an advertisement for the business as "E. Grover, St Mary's Road, Ealing – Builder, Undertaker, etc., House and Estate Agent. Estates Managed, rents collected". It also stated that the business had been established over a century. (2) The newspaper also announced on the 2nd April 1892 that Mr S. Dyer of the Broadway Depository purchased the business carried on by Messrs. Grovers and Tidy, auctioneers at the Auction Hall. The newspaper wrote that it was interesting as the business was long standing, one of the oldest in the town, and would in future be carried on under the energetic management of a Mr Priest. (3) It is likely that the transfer of business to Mr Dyer was the auctioneer part of the business as the Grover firm continued to advertise as an Undertaking and Building business following the transfer.

Wisteria Cottage and the business yard of the Grover business was near the "New Inn" which has since been rebuilt and the signage above it today gives the date as 1897. (Illustration 3) During the period when the Grover family ran the funeral business the Inn was a 'posting house' and coaches left regularly for London from the Inn and local carriers ran between Brentford and London. The Inn was a centre for local business and would have been very near to the yard at Wisteria Cottage. In 1844 the Grovers' cash book shows that work was carried out at the Inn for eight pounds ten shillings and two pence. (4)

Posting arrangements were managed by a man with the name of Ives. The 'New Inn' was connected by a glass corridor to the 'Assembly Rooms' which was a place for local entertainment. The 'Assembly Rooms' were taken over in 1869 by the Grover family for use as a furniture showroom and warehouse. (5)

During most of the period covered here (c.1790-1890) married women could not own property and the male line dominated in this as in most other trades. However, the women's role in the funeral business was of primary importance and may have gone by almost unnoticed in the local society. It has been shown that following the death of their husbands both Frances Grover and Eliza Martha assumed more responsibility for the business. The 1851 census showed Frances Grover aged 27 was identified as a carpenter and undertaker employing three men, while her husband William was a licensed victualler. (6) William and Elizabeth also had as lodgers three casual labourers, one carpenter, one greengrocer and one bricklayer's labourer. It is likely that some of these men assisted with the funeral business as and when required.

There is also a will which shows another Mary Grover (not known to be related to the Ealing Grover family) living in the parish of Saint Saviours, Southwark who was also determined to ensure that her daughter was secure financially. Written in January 1721 she "give and bequeath to my daughter Mary Grover all that I have and possess whether goods of chattels or whatsoever else doth both belong to me. After my decease.... And if my daughter Mary Grover dyes before she marry or arrive to the age of eighteen years. Then my will is. That my brother John Grover's children shall have one half of what is left to be divided amongst them as he shall think fit and the other half of what shall be then left I give and bequeath to William Walker and Jane Walker, son and daughter of William Walker, distiller to be equally divided between them". It is interesting to see that Mary Grover was not only determined her daughter would be secure, but she was also willing to bequeath equally to both the daughter as well as the son of William Walker. (7)

Within living memory the layers out of the dead in labouring communities were traditionally women and it has been shown that this activity also tended to run in the family as part of an unspoken community support system to help neighbours and attend to the practical details. (8) According to Elizabeth Roberts:

"Laying out did something to demystify death, the bereaved had something practical and detailed to think about, for example what the dead person would wear. Layers out were practical women often humorous, always kindly. Some were paid, some accepted presents, others refused all recompense, seeing the laying out as part of their neighbourly, perhaps religious duty". (9)

The skills required by an undertaker were similar to those of the layer out – practicality, strength, dexterity, sensitivity and lack of fear. (10)

In addition to these attributes the undertaker would have had to be adaptable for he encountered customers on a day to day basis who were placing orders for domestic carpentry or building work but he also had to be able to communicate with them diplomatically often at the most distressing time in their lives when they required his services as an undertaker. This certainly applied to the Grover family of undertakers / builders / carpenters. One family historian commenting on this aspect in his own family history in the late eighteenth century states that:

"To an extent perhaps greater than any other craftsman, the carpenter was closely and intimately involved in the life of the entire parish". (11)

Marriages into other undertaking families occurred frequently. The social and business contacts which existed between the trading families in the local community undoubtedly contributed to this. Members of the Grover family married into families from the local upholstery and cabinet making businesses and they also had dealings with the Nye family of Undertakers (although they did not marry into it) by regularly hiring palls, cloaks and scarves needed for funerals from them. (12)

Undertakers combined the work of other business, such as carpentry work with the funeral business especially in rural areas such as Ealing. Urban funerals were often elaborate and costly compared to funerals held in rural communities. There lay a big difference between the funerals of the upper classes and the working classes and the poor. The contrast changed with time and whereas the funerals of those from the upper echelons of society became simpler, those of the tradesmen and artisans became more extravagant. An analysis of funeral costs in the 1840s were published in a report by Edwin

Chadwick in 1843 entitled The Practice of Internment in Towns. The report indicated clearly how the cost was related to the social standing of the deceased person and his or her family. (13)

The success of the business also depended on the family business's ability, skills and readiness to diversify their trades and skills and of course that there was at least one son willing and able to learn the skills to continue the family business line. That women played a role in the business, as in the case of the Grover family could suggest that other undertakers' wives or widows may also have contributed their labour and skills in the day to day running of the business.

WHITE HART & COFFIN

Illustration 1a - Undertaker Shop Signs c. 1680-c.1740. (a) William Boyce, at Ye Whight Hart & Coffin, in ye Grate Ould Bayley, Near Newgeat. c. 1680.

11

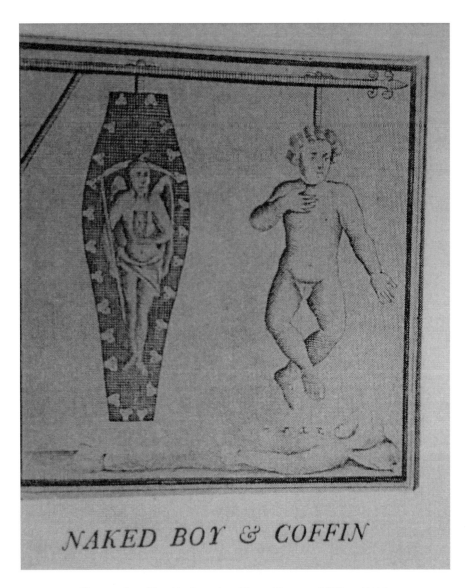

Illustration 1b - Undertaker Shop Signs c. 1680-c.1740.
William Grinley, at Ye sign of ye Naked Boy & Coffin,
at ye Lower Corner of Fleet Lane. c. 1730.

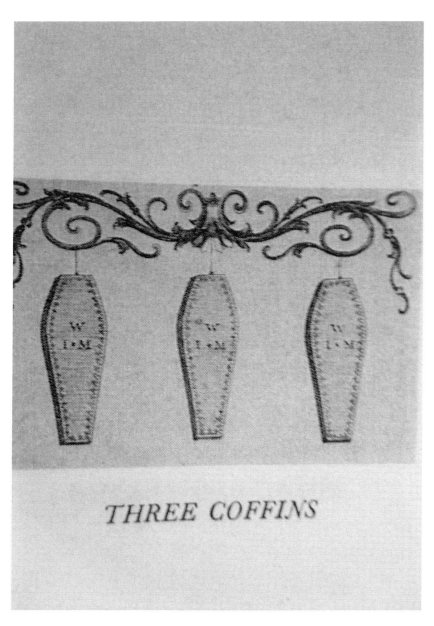

Illustration 1c - Undertaker Shop Signs c. 1680-c.1740.
Issac Whitchurch, removed from Fleet Lane to the Three Coffins.

13

Illustration 2 - Thorn Place.

Illustration 3 - Photograph of the New Inn Public House, May 2017.

Illustration 4 - Wisteria Cottage, Ealing

Illustration 5 - Employees of J. & F. Grover in the yard at Wisteria Cottage, Ealing.

Illustration 6 – Postcard of St Mary's Road Ealing.

Chapter 3: The Work and Business Organisation of the Grover Funeral Business

This chapter looks at the organisation and clientele as seen in the day to day running of a family based undertakers (who were also carpenters, builders and blind makers) working during the mid-nineteenth century. It examines traditional mixed business at a time when the specialist urban funeral director, trading his wares on every High Street was starting to emerge.

This has been made possible by the use of abstracts from J. & F. Grover's cash book (1841-1847), their correspondence contained in the estimate book (27th June 1859 - 29th July 1868) and their ledger of business transactions (1847-1855). This ledger of business transactions (1847-1855) has been examined in more detail to provide an insight into the social status of the Grovers' clientele and to establish and assess what proportion of the work actually consisted of Funerals. The Grover family undertaking business methods to increase trade by tendering for contracts and advertising has also been looked at in this booklet.

The business was established at Wisteria Cottage close to the parish church of St Mary's South Ealing. (1) (Illustration 4) Wisteria Cottage was formerly known as the "Old Tithe Barn" and remained until it was demolished after the Second World War and even at that stage descendants of the Grover family still lived there. (2) It was situated in the area which is now occupied by St Mary's Court on St Mary's Road, South Ealing. Probably as a result of the residents' skills and knowledge of the building and carpentry trade the arrangement of rooms was uneven and apparently haphazard. (3) The Cottage had apparently been painted many times by local artists and it would be interesting to find where these paintings are now located. (4) The building also had the advantage of a large yard conveniently situated next to the "New Inn" where Grover employees could take their refreshment. The yard provided space for materials required in the running of the business, although it is not known whether horses were stabled there or elsewhere. (Illustration 5) Some of Grover's business would have consisted of passing trade, such as packing belongings and furniture because the business was adjacent to the "New Inn" and nearby coaches left for London. (4) The location of the firm was an important factor in the growth and success of the business as it was in close proximity to the parish churchyard which meant that the transportation of coffins for the service and burial would have been relatively easy and its' location at the centre point of the village would have been advantageous for other work as well as funerals. (Illustration 6, 7 & 8)

Ealing in the mid nineteenth century was primarily an agricultural community. Regular and close contacts must have existed between all the local tradesmen and their clients. In Masons' Directory for 1853 John Grover was described as a carpenter and Mrs Frances Grover as a builder, rather than undertakers. There were several other carpenters and builders as well as three listed undertakers also in Ealing so business competition and a certain degree of co-operation has been found to have existed between the firms.

The Middlesex County Times, including the Brentford Gazette, which was founded in 1866 carried trade advertisements for J. & F. Grover and other Ealing undertakers. For example, the undertaker   A . J.

Wilkins had the following advertisement published in the Middlesex County Times Saturday 5th January 1867:

"Practical cabinet Maker, Upholsterer and Undertaker. Private residence 1 Cavendish Villa, The Grove, Ealing, A.J.W. returns his sincere thanks to those who favoured him with their patronage since commencing business as above and having had 14 years practical experience in a First Class London house, trusts by punctuality and good workmanship, combined with moderate charges to receive a further share of patronage, which it will be his consistent standing to deserve. Cabinet furniture of every description made to order and dry wood guaranteed, ladies needlework tastefully mounted. Funerals performed with economy, carpets taken up, beaten and re-laid. Packing cases made to order on the shortest notice. Estimates given for general repairs. Workshops back of Mr B. Hayles. Pharmaceutical Chemist, Broadway". (6)

Trade cards were also becoming more widely used by the undertaking trade as the century went on, along with the increase in memorial cards and black edged bill heads. (Illustration 9a & 9b) The undertakers' shop often advertised wares by the use of a painted signboard, the shop front black lettered, picked out in gold and silver. Often a richly decorated coffin was displayed in the shop window and when the number of styles in coffins increased later on in the century, the various styles were shown in the shop or as models used for the dual purpose of also taking to the houses of the rich clientele. (7)

Competition between the different undertaking firms existed in the previous decade when on the 19th April 1834 James Grover submitted a tender for the contract of supplying coffins for the workhouse, in small and large sizes. (8) Listed below are the undertakers who were competing for the contract and their costs:

	Small	Large
Mr J. Grainger	5/6	12/9
Mr John Sims	5/3	11/6
Mr James Grover	5/6	12/4
Mr Henry Ezard	6/0	13/6
George Maberbey	6/3	12/0

Mr John Sims obtained the contract. James Grover submitted his costs six months later when he reduced the estimate for the small size coffins to five shillings and the large ones to eleven shillings. However, shrewd businessman Mr Sims had likewise reduced his costs to the same as Mr Grover and yet again, for one reason or the other, obtained the contract. Not to be beaten, Mr Grover submitted his costs again on 4th April 1835, this time only competing with John Sims and Mr. W. P. Grainger. Both Grainger and Grover had estimates of five shillings and eleven shillings. Needless to say Sims again cut costs, this time to four shillings and nine pence and ten shillings and six pence and received the contract yet again! James Grover must have regretted not submitting a tender six months later as this time Sims increased his costs to five shillings and to eleven shillings three pence and rival Mr Grainger keeping his costs the same as the Grovers obtained the business to supply the coffins for the burial of the Poor of the Parish. Tradesmen such as Mr Henry Ezard and Mr J. Grainger clearly aimed to achieve the maximum profit possible when they submitted their first tenders for providing the coffins to dispose of the Ealing Poor.

During the period 1847-1855 a total number of 721 business transactions were entered in the 680 pages of J. & F. Grover's ledger and are listed in Appendix 1. Funerals accounted for only a small percentage - only 83 - and are listed in Appendix 2. Approximately 220 names are listed in the ledger (1847-1855) as paying for work done by the Grover business and these people are listed in Appendix 3.

By comparing the names of clients in the Index of Grover's Ledger (1847-1855) to the names and addresses listed under the Gentry and Traders in Masons' Directory for Ealing 1853 it is possible to establish the social groups able to afford the services of the Grover family, either in their role as undertakers, builders, blind makers or carpenters.   These families have been identified and listed in Appendix 3. Such a comparison by surname can only be based upon assumptions until further research is carried out on families living in Ealing during the nineteenth century.

Approximately one third of the local Ealing Gentry (58 out of the 180 listed in Masons' Directory) used Grover business for work and just one quarter (63) of the Traders required work done by the Grover business during this period. (9) Some of the names in the ledger are not listed in the Directory and may have come from those of the labouring men and women, although it is more than likely that they were from the Gentry or "Traders" from outside the area. Two such examples are E. D. Harman Esq. of Gerrards Cross and Welch Esq. of 13 Wyndham Place, Bryanston Square in Central London.

It can be ascertained from these figures that the Grover family provided a reasonably priced and reliable service for the trade to be as thriving as it apparently appeared to be. The Grover family firm of undertakers had been established since at least the early 1820s, probably before 1792, and by the period examined here they must have established a respectable reputation judging by the regularity with which their services were required.

The cash book is dated 1841-1847 although there are brief entries for 1828 and 1839. The contents and condition of the book are such that they may well reflect the rather rudimentary organisation of some of the undertakers and builders at that period, although it is only fair to say that many of the pages may have been cut at a later date. However, it is very much what it claims to be – a cash book containing the cost and payment of work done by the Grover family and some details regarding the nature of the work. It not only concerns funerals but also general carpentry and building work as well as blind making.

The most lucrative work carried out by the Grover business during this period was for a Mr Thompson, who actually hired the firm on seventeen separate occasions. (10) His bill for 1844 amounted to the princely sum of eight hundred and sixty pounds eleven shillings and six pence with his hot houses accounting for five hundred and thirty six pounds thirteen shillings and four pence of the total and his garden fee to Christmas one hundred and thirteen pounds eleven shillings and four pence. A Mr Thomson made part payment of his fee by "foods" amounting to a small fraction of the total amount of forty one pounds two pence.

This system of payment in kind for work carried out, including funerals, occurs frequently throughout the cash book and is partly a reflection of the organisation of a small, family business.   It is also perhaps an indication of the structure of the local economy during this period.   The system of exchanging goods for services rendered probably proved to be more economical and labour saving for the Grover family in the long run.   For example, the part payment of bills by timber which J. Atkinson made in 1842 for the fee of two pounds was undoubtedly advantageous to both parties. (11) Later on in the century Britain's forest wealth declined and white elm had to be imported from Ontario, Canada for use as coffins. (12)   Several examples of the payments in kind made are briefly mentioned below:

p.9 1843	£	s	d
J. IBBOTSON FEE			
By oak and chestnut	3	10	0
By 2 loads of hay at 3/10/0	8	15	0
By 2 water butts	1	0	0
Of a total fee of	63	10	0
p.67 1842			
MISS CUTHBERTSON			
Paid by sale of furniture	75	15	6
Including fee for funeral			
and other work	61	19	0

1842

MR SQUIRE

By old bedstead door		8	0

p. 158 14th May 1843

MR H. CRISP

Fee for funeral		7	9
3 Debit cash		10	0
By roasting pig		9	9

The human element also comes across in the following:

MR J. ATLEE

Produced receipt dated 1837	16	0	0
Produced 2 memoran	10	0	0
demands 5.00 each			
Allowed on Mr Gordon's	5	10	0
advertisement			
Allowed for bricks	10	2	11
MR ATLEE disputing the	1	6	0
fee for the same			

26

Suffice to say that the adjoining page giving details of payment by Mr Atlee were torn out.

Apart from the undertaking side of the business the other work carried out by the Grover family firm provides a fascinating glimpse into the domestic history of those Victorians who could afford to hire their services. Details concerning the buildings and furnishings to some of the Ealing houses were listed and would be of interest to a researcher examining the history of their Ealing house or looking for an ancestor in this area.

One of the most unusual and saddest jobs carried out by the firm during this period was the installation of a padded room paid for by a Miss Dence. (13) It included "making of strong deal frames, canvassing and padding and ditto with strong brown ticking and making, fitting, glazing and hanging sashes. Making, fitting and padding and covering ditto and walls and fixing frames, hanging wire gauze blinds to windows". Whoever was the resident of this room was at least saved the even worse fate of the workhouse.

Some of the work carried out by the business during this period included putting up verandas, pulling down the old Rectory House, repairing chairs, making boxes, taking out cupboards, packing furniture and laying carpets. The constant battle with dirt and bugs also becomes apparent: on the 23rd August 1847 Dr Tattersall was charged three pounds threepence for the taking down, cleaning and putting up of bedstead, the price included the carpenters and bug poison. (14)

Typical of England's population at the time which was still mainly rural, was the keeping of animals and the ledger reveals the construction of work on rabbit boxes, bee hives, pigsties, duck ponds, stables and hen houses.

Another regular source of work was the upholstery side of the business, such as making up cushions, needlework boxes and mattresses. Mrs Burton had a "new needlework cushion, padded and covered with silk six shillings and six pence". (15) This skill is closely related to the craft required by the undertaker in his preparation of the coffin before burial and often found as a trade carried out simultaneously with Undertaking.

Rather poignantly Mrs Smallman employed the Grover business for four days during the summer of 1850 preparing and fixing the spout by the side of her house, making and fixing new oak frame grating into the cellar and repairing safe. (16)   She paid one pound seven shillings and five pence. The following winter her name was back in the ledger book again with the bill of fifty eight pounds three pence for her burial in an elm inside coffin, a strong outside coffin and a strong lead coffin, her idea of keeping her possessions safe had extended beyond her life and into death to protect her own corpse, possibly for fear of the body snatchers. (17)

Work was also carried out for the Churchwardens, for the upkeep of the parish fire engine, new handles on cricket bats for the Ealing Cricket Club and work on the vaults. A "recipe" was even written down for whitewash paint which was popular in interior decorating at the time: "A beautiful cream colour may be made by adding three pounds of yellow ochre or a good pearl colour of lead colour by the addition of a lump of ivory black". (18)

J. & F. Grover arranged only eighty three funerals between 1847 and 1855 and the income obtained from most funerals varied according to the requirements of the family making the arrangements for the burial of a member of their family or a friend. The irregular and unpredictable nature of the funeral business meant that the building, carpentry, blind making and other miscellaneous work formed the basis for the business in the years between 1847-1855 and probably continued to do so in later years.

The success of J. & F. Grover business in surviving the economic depression of the 1840s – the "Hungry Forties" was largely the result of efficient business organisation by the family. The diversity of the trade and the central location of the firm in a suburban area with a growing middle class residency was also a contributory factor. The firm was typical of the village carpenter, combining his craft with other related skills and adjusting to the increasing demands for his labour.

Illustration 7 - Postcard of St Mary's Old Church, Ealing c. 1906.

Illustration 8 - Photograph of St Mary's Church, May 2017.

Illustration 9a - Trade Card of the Grover family business, Ealing.

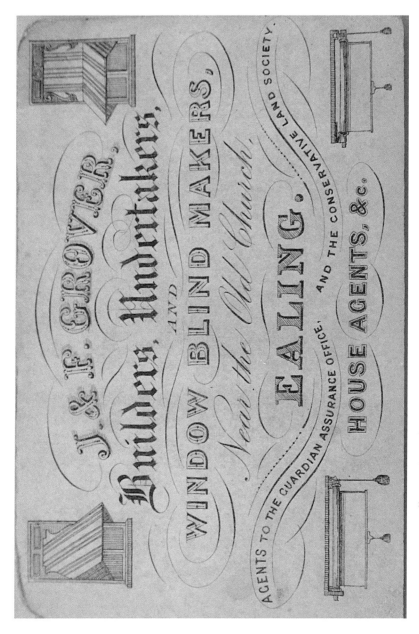

Illustration 9b - Trade Card of the Grover family business, Ealing.

33

Illustration 10 - Photograph of the Lychgate at St Mary's Church, May 2017.

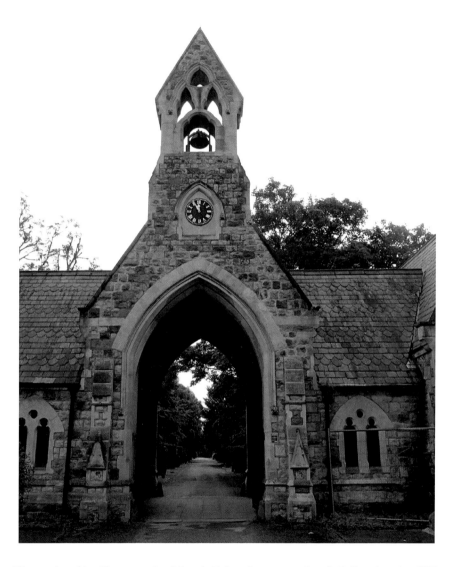

Illustration 11 - Photograph of South Ealing Cemetery, South Ealing, London W5

Illustration 12 - Photograph of an inscription to Reverend Relton on the Lychgate St Mary's Church, May 2017. (2)

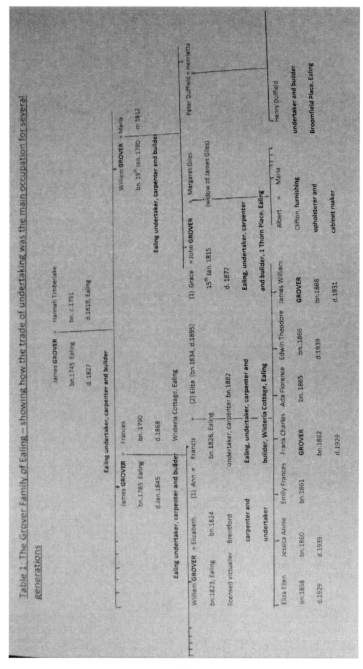

Table 1 The Grover Family of Ealing - showing how the trade of undertaking was the main occupation for several generations

Chapter 4: The Grovers as Undertakers

This chapter continues to examine the funeral work of the Grover firm set against a background of development in the undertaking trade in general. The business ledger shows that eighty three funerals were arranged by the Grover business between 1847 and 1855 and are listed in Appendix 2. As in the previous chapter, a comparison between Gentry and Traders listed in Mason's Directory of 1853 has provided information about the social grouping of the customers who had paid for the services from the Grover business. (1) Fourteen members of the local Gentry and twenty nine members of the Ealing Traders used the firm to arrange their family funeral during these years. The following is a typical funeral for a member of the Ealing gentry:

The funeral of Mr Chas. Starkey 16th March 1847:

For his funeral at Ealing a strong elm made coffin, pitched,

lined and ruffled with superfine cambric

	1	15	0

A superfine cambric winding sheet with mattress and pillow

	1	10	0

Bearing in coffin and putting in corpse

		4	6

A strong extra size lead coffin

7	0	0

A lead plate with inscription

3	6

A strong elm outside coffin covered with best black

Cloth ornamented with three rows of best black

 nails, four pairs of handles, glory and New Angel drops

 and plate with inscription

6	6	0

Bearing in coffin, removing out of window and soldiering down

10	0

Use of the best velvet pall

7	6

Porters silk dresses and poles

7	6

Six mourners best cloaks

9	0

Two porters and twelve bearers attendance

4	4	0

Five best crepe hatbands 5/0. One best silk hatband

1	2

Six pair of kid gloves for mourners

| | 2 | 19 | 6 |

Best silk hatband 12/0 and gloves 3/9 for each

minister, clerk and surgeon and pair of best kid

gloves for Mr Thomson

| | 2 | 11 | 0 |

Attendance of undertaker with silk hatband and gloves

| | | 7 | 6 |

Paid fees as per bill

| | 1 | 7 | 0 |

Refreshments for fourteen men

| | 1 | 1 | 0 |

Gave grave diggers

| | | 1 | 6 |

The total cost of Mr Starkey's funeral was

| | 31 | 11 | 6 |

(2)

The most expensive funeral carried out by the business during the period covered in this booklet was for the sum of sixty six pounds eighteen shillings and six pence for the burial of Mrs Jane Tattersall, the wife of Dr James Tattersall, a member of the Ealing Gentry.

However, most of the Grover fee charges were below eight pounds which included disbursements of burial fees and costs for the sexton, vicar, gravedigger and clerk. This meant that the profit made by the firm would really have been quite low. These fees are included at the back of the Grovers' ledger (1847-1855). Funeral charges varied according to the status of the client, the location and the complexity of the funeral.

Edwin Chadwick commenting on funeral costs in the early 1840s wrote that the English gentry paid from one hundred and fifty pounds to one thousand pounds while an ordinary member of the professions or respectable tradesperson paid about seventy pounds. (3)

Located in the largely residential area of Ealing the firm of J. & F. Grover was experienced in the organisation of funerals for both the gentry and the tradespeople of the village and the surrounding area. The following is an example of the funeral of a respectable tradesman: - C. N. Atlee of the Academy, Ealing Park School and is described here:

"Funeral of the above respected gentleman. A notice of whose lamented death with a short memoir we published in our last week's impression, took place on Thursday last amidst a large and respectable assembly of the principal inhabitants of the village at Ealing cemetery.

The mournful cortege assembled at the residence of the deceased at Ealing Park and was arranged as follows:

Churchwardens of Ealing

The Overseers

The old inhabitants and principal tradesmen

The pupils of Byron House School

Pall Bearers   The Body   Pall Bearers

Members of the Local Board   Members of the Local Board

Two mourning coaches with family and near relatives of the deceased"

According to this report this funeral was the first to be carried out in the church following the restoration of St Mary's by the architect Samuel Sanders Teulon (1812-1873). "The coffin was met at the entry to the church by the Reverend E.W. Relton M.A. Vicar of Ealing who read in a most earnest and impressive manner the service of the Church of England, after which the body was taken to its' final resting place in the village testified the respect in which the deceased was held by partially closing their establishments during the funeral". (4) Reverend Relton probably met the coffin at the lychgate which still stands at the front of St Mary's Church, Ealing. (Illustration 10)

Although an estimate published in the Lancet in 1835 indicated that the death rate for children had been halved between 1750 and 1830, the infant mortality rate was still high and this was reflected in the funerals contained in the ledgers of the firm. (5) The following is an example of one funeral carried out by the Grover family for the local trader Mr H. Crisp, letter carrier of Church Lane, Ealing:

"A strong elm coffin planed and ornamented with single row of white nails, handles, angles and flower and plate inscription the inside lined with cambric. The use of two hoods and scarfs and small pall". (6)

It is likely that the attendance of the undertaker and bearers was not required at this funeral. Local men were employed for other funerals and also for work on the building side of the business. In 1841 one carpenter's apprentice lived with the Grover family at Ealing and by 1851 Francis Grover is known to have employed at least four men. (7) The Grover firm's proximity to the churchyard meant that coachmen and horses were seldom needed. A photograph of the yard at Wisteria Cottage (Illustration 5) shows several workmen present. It is likely that the employment of at least one dozen men would have been required on many funerals, probably hired in on a casual basis during this period. Fourteen men were employed on the funeral of Chas. Starkey and the executors of Starkey's will were charged six shillings for each man. This did not include their refreshments which amounted to one shilling and six pence each. There is uncertainty regarding the assessment of real wages during the nineteenth century, but is generally agreed that the rural wages for men for the first three decades of the period could be as low as nine shillings per week. (8) By 1867 a general labourer was probably receiving approximately fourteen shillings for one week's work. (9) Grover himself either personally supervised the funeral or employed a trusted senior member of his workforce to the role of undertaker, charging seven shillings and six pence for this task.

Most of the funerals arranged by the business between 1847 and 1855 were burials in Ealing. In December 1852 the committee appointed at a Vestry meeting obtained an addition to the burial ground and submitted their statement of accounts to the subscribers, listing Mr H. Grover as donating five shillings. (10) A new cemetery was opened up to accommodate the needs of Ealing's growing population on the South Ealing Road and was consecrated by the Bishop of London on 10th August 1861. (11) It had been designed by the local architect Charles Jones (1830-1913) who also designed Ealing Town Hall. (Illustration 11)

Ealing was undergoing increasing urbanisation and by 1871 the population had increased to 5,000. The Great Western Railway opened a main line from Paddington to the West in 1838 with stations at Ealing and nearby Hanwell and by the 1850s parts of Ealing had obtained a gas supply too. It became "one of the most fashionable areas west of London" to live in, and an increasingly middle class society began to develop. (12) The parish church of St Mary's was enlarged and almost entirely rebuilt between 1866 and 1872 and a lychgate erected as a memorial to Reverend Relton, the vicar responsible for remodelling the church. (13) (Illustration 12) Messrs. J & F. Grover are known to have subscribed three pounds three shillings to the Parish Church Restoration Fund in 1864. (14) John Grover was a member of the Parish vestry and attended a meeting in March 1875 and proposed that a poor rate of one shilling and four pence be made, which was carried unanimously. (15) Mr Francis was nominated as Overseer of the Poor on the 31st March 1874. (16) In spite of these changes residents of Ealing still wanted and indeed were able to be buried within the churchyard during a period when areas of inner London were struggling with the problem of burying their dead in overcrowded churchyards. Between 1866 to 1875 and the funerals carried out by the Grover family were predominantly still village based and the new cemeteries such as Kensal Green and Hanwell, Kensington Cemetery were not yet used to the same extent. (17)

In general the cemeteries owned by joint stock companies such as Kensal Green (founded in 1833) and public cemeteries gave an impetus to the growth and specialization of the undertaking trade with an increasing number located in London and the immediate environs. Trade directories covering this period reflect this growth. There were 160 undertakers listed in Pigots Directory of 1822/23. (18) By 1852 there were 368 undertakers listed in the Post Office Directory and this number had risen to 434 in 1875. (19)

Burial in the fashionable suburban cemeteries often involved the regular use of horses and elaborate hearses and coaches, and even the increased use of the expanding railway network. Brookwood cemetery, Woking and the Great Northern, New Southgate were served by their own stations from London. (20)

The ornate funerals, memorials, mementoes and all the associated pageantry became generally adopted by those who wanted this kind of funeral and who could afford these extra embellishments. It has been suggested that these developments were partially the result of the 1832 Anatomy Act, which effectively destroyed the gangs of body snatchers by the legal provision of corpses to the anatomical schools from unclaimed workhouse inmates. It seems clear that "with the demise of body snatchers both the anxiety associated with protecting the dead and the emotional / financial investment in a grave safe from the body snatchers, transmuted into and fed from serving to signal the achievement of respectable and safe burial". (21) The historian, Ruth Richardson goes on to explain the simultaneous growth in burial clubs and friendly societies. "Fear of death on the parish", she suggests, "promoted the purchase of death insurance on a mass scale and helps explain both the mushroom growth of friendly and burial societies from the 1830's onwards and the high expenditure on death among the very poor". (22)

Payments to these organisations were often the first to be curtailed if the wage-earner's ability to work was cut through sickness or other misfortune. Some other groups such as costermongers and cabbies also resorted to community action to finance the burial. (23)

The period covered by the Grover business records saw marked changes occurring within the London undertaking trade. They reflect a general shift in social, economic and demographic patterns of the nation at large. The Grover business moved in tandem with these developments becoming a successful business providing for the needs and demands of Ealing residents.

Chapter 5: The Victorian Funeral and the Undertaking Business 1830-1900

The Grover family undertaking business was set up during the period of England's first industrialisation and was influenced by the national, economic, social and demographic trends. However, the pattern of development in the undertaking trade was also shaped by changing attitudes to death, grief and burial in the Victorian period. At first, funerals and burials became increasingly elaborate as extra precautions were introduced to protect the corpse from the body snatchers. Some of these changes such as double and triple coffins were continued after the problem of grave robbery had been resolved by the Anatomy Act of 1832. The historian and author, Ruth Richardson has shown how this piece of legislation also played a more generalised part in changing attitudes to death and burial, particularly among the poor.   The avoidance of death in the workhouse and likely dissection by the Anatomist became embedded and feared in the consciousness of the poor.   This consequently contributed to the demand for a 'decent burial'. Burial in style, with an elaborate memorial in one of the new cemeteries, a lengthy mourning period and all the accompanying funeral etiquette was the pinnacle of dying for the middle classes.

After 1832 it became of equal importance among the labouring classes too. They began to adopt the lengthy mourning period and dress which were already rigidly adhered to by the other classes of society. The Victorian male was usually dressed in dark colours and black whether in mourning or not and did not suffer to the same extent as the bereaved woman who was forced by inbuilt public displeasure, to wear the unfashionable, rough, heavy and restrictive garments. (1) Betram Puckle indicates the social pressures put on people to conform to mourning dress. He relates the story of a young servant girl married to a house painter. Within a year of the marriage he tragically fell from a ladder and was killed. She bought a cheap little black dress and simple straw hat for the funeral and her former employer had commended her for this modest outlay. A few days later he met the young girl swathed in crepe, her poor little face only half visible under a hideous widow's bonnet, complete with streamers and veil. When asked why she had made these purchases she explained that her neighbours had made her life unbearable and had said that "if I would not wear a bonnet, it proved we were never married". (2)

In spite of the seemingly superficial mourning rituals which became ever more popular from the mid-century, it has been suggested that many of these customs provided " a valuable function in rallying the support network of family, friends and neighbours and enabling them to operate effectively within a dignified framework". (3) The author, Pat Jalland has examined the correspondence and diaries of more than sixty upper class and middle class families from 1850 until the early decades of the twentieth century where the loss of a spouse has been experienced. Her study revealed very few cases of chronic grief, the same type of grief suffered by Queen Victoria for at least twelve years following the death of Prince Albert. She has also found that the widows seemed to cope more readily with their grief than some groups of widows examined by psychologists in the following years. She suggested that the possible explanation for this may be the more effective support of family, friends and religious beliefs which were available in the period before the outbreak of the First World War. She also suggested that the nineteenth century mourning rituals may have met the psychological needs of the bereaved by decreasing the terrifying aspects of death and structuring the grieving process within "a coherent set of customs". (4) However, the strict code of conduct and long period of mourning which was adopted by Victorian widows following the example of Queen Victoria after the death of Prince Albert must have been restrictive and difficult for the widow to move on from her loss. Victorian widows were expected to adopt the oppressive rules of widowhood – deep mourning, for at least a year, along with the obligatory dress code of black clothes and veil. The veil was often made of crepe which affected some wearers with asthma, catarrh and cataracts because of the black dyes. Following the first year of mourning the widow was dressed in "secondary mourning" for another nine months and allowed to wear some white on the cuffs and collars. (5)

All these changes and this mix of circumstances lay behind the commercial success of the Grover family of undertakers as well as a large number of similar family undertaking businesses across the London area. Other undertakers included the long established firms founded during the eighteenth and early nineteenth centuries who had achieved a high status as experienced funeral businesses, often providing the very elaborate and detailed funerals for royalty and the aristocracy. One example is the firm of Messrs. France and Banting, the Crown undertakers responsible for the funeral arrangements of Caroline of Brunswick, George IV's wife. (5)

Large undertaking companies such as The London Necropolis Company also responded to, and encouraged, the desire for large scale funerals with all their finery and ostentatious trimmings. At the same time these needs were met by a growing number of small undertaking firms which had developed from other related trades, such as carpentry and upholstery and already situated in prime positions on the busy main High Streets. Many were aware of the reputation as a "Dismal Trader" often exploiting the fears and aspirations of his clients. An example of this is the daughter in a London suburb who arranged the funeral of a parent and when she chose an elm coffin without ornamentation the horrified undertaker said "Elm, you can't have anything but polished oak in a road like this". (6) Associated crafts such as monumental masonry, the black crepe industry and hearse building saw great changes and growth to supply the needs of the funeral business.

The success of the family run funeral business was also dependent upon there being at least one son who had the ability and inclination to assume the responsibility for the running of the business. Even with the knowledge that the high mortality rate meant the average Victorian was no stranger to death the young undertaker still had to be able to cope with sometimes distressing causes of death or corpses in any state of decomposition. He would have been constantly on call, even during the night and he would have been able to use tact and diplomacy with clientele from all social classes at a difficult time for them. He would also have to attend to the business accounts and deal with the detail of a funeral arrangement. Examination of the Grover firm's records indicates that women members of the family also handled some of the responsibility. Some funeral firms also provided the 'funeral feast' and the preparation of the food and drink would have been done mainly by female members of the family.

As has been shown there were often connections between families engaged in the funeral business as well as in related trades. There were strong links between the carpentry trade and the funeral business and the Grover family business records show that in many ways the traditional idea of the village undertaker / carpenter still existed but did change and develop from the 1830s onwards.

Located in the centre of an expanding village, close to the parish church of St Mary's, the Grover firm expanded as a result of the changes taking place nationally - both economically, demographically and socially - including changing attitudes to death and burial. Situated on the outskirts of London, with increasing expansion and rail travel links to central London, the Grover firm continued to offer Ealing residents a wider range of skills into the twentieth century. The firm succeeded in retaining many of the attributes common to the pre-industrial village undertaker / carpenter and adapted the business to the changing characteristics of an urban based society. This type of small undertaking concern which served the needs of the local community was typical throughout the country. The 'Celebration of Death' and the 'Disposal of the Dead' has been a major preoccupation of mankind from the earliest time. During the period looked at here, mainly through the ledgers of the Grover funeral business, it has reflected the work of professional undertaker working at a local level at a period of urbanisation and change. A period when the pressures on local churchyards, particularly in urban areas, were reaching crisis levels and the development of municipal cemeteries were taking place.

Notes

Notes to Chapter 1 : The Undertaking Trade and Burial of the Poor 1650-1830

(1) Julian Litten, "Journeys to Paradise: Funerary Transport 1600-1850", Genealogists Magazine, Vol.23, (1990), p.174.

(2) Litten, "Journeys", p.174

(3) Ibid, p.173.

(4) Ibid, p.173.

(5) Tony Walter, Funerals and How to Improve Them, (Kent: Hodder & Stoughton, 1990), p.76.

(6) Broadside, London c.1720, Guildhall Library, Broadside 24.100

(7) Litten, "Journeys", p.174.

(8) Ibid, p.174.

(9) Inventory of Thomas Phill, 11th February 1717, L.M.A DL/AM/P1/01/1719/003.

(10) Apprentice Indenture of Joseph Taylor, 3rd July 1814, L.M.A DRO/020/E/03/001.

(11) Fred Bush, "Undertakers 1799-1854 : extracted from the Burial Register of Wesley's Chapel, City Road". (London: London and North Middlesex Family History Society 1990) mf.

(12) Elizabeth Roberts, "The Lancashire Way of Death", in Ralph Houlbrooke, ed. Death, Ritual and Bereavement (London: Routledge, 1989), p.191.

(13) Roberts, "Lancashire Way", p.192.

(14)Rowland Parker, <u>The Common Stream</u> (St Albans, Herts : Granada Publishing Limited, 1976), p.191.

(15)Litten, "Journeys", p.175.

(16)Ruth Richardson, <u>Death Dissection and the Destitute</u> (London: Fontana, 1971), p.81.

(17)Hugh Meller, <u>London Cemeteries</u> (Amersham: Avebury Publishing Company, 1981), p.8.

(18)Richardson, <u>Death</u>, p.61.

(19)Meller, <u>London</u>, p.11.

Notes to Chapter 2 : The Funeral Business as a Family Tradition

(1)   Eric. H. Whittledon, The Grover Family of Ealing (Ealing: Ealing Museum of Art and History Society, 1982). Further information on the history of the Grover family is obtained from this book, unless otherwise stated.

(2)   Middlesex County Times, 14th May 1892, Ealing Local History Library 1517/4.

(3)   Middlesex County Times, 2nd April 1892, Ealing Local History Library 1511/6.

(4)   J & F Grover Cash Book, 1841-1847; L.M.A. ACC/0694/001.

(5)   Whittledon, The Grover, p.7.

(6)   Ealing census, 1851, T.NA.

(7)   Mary Grover will; L.M.A. DW/PC/05/1722/015

(8)   Roberts, "Lancashire Way", p.194.

(9)   Ibid, p.191.

(10) Richardson, <u>Death</u>, p.21.

(11) Peter Sanders, <u>The Simple Annals</u> (Gloucester: Alan Sutton, 1989), pp.34, 35.

(12) J & F Grover Ledger, 1866-1878; L.M.A. ACC/0694/004.

(13) May, Trevor, <u>The Victorian Undertaker</u> (Buckinghamshire: Shire Publications Ltd, 2007).

Notes to Chapter 3 : The Work and Business Organisation of the Grover Funeral Business

(1) Whittledon, The Grover, p.6.

(2) Ibid, p.6.

(3) Ibid, p.6.

(4) Ibid, p.6.

(5) Kate McEwan, Ealing Walkabout (London : Pulse Publications, 1993), p.40.

(6) Middlesex County Times, Saturday 5 January 1867.

(7) Barbara Jones, Design for Death (London : Andre Deutsch Limited, 1967), p.111.

(8) Ealing Overseers of the Poor. Tenders for contracts, 1834-1836; L.M.A ACC/2208/E/123.

(9) Mason's Directory (1853)

(10) J & F Grover Cash book 1841-1847; L.M.A. ACC/0694/001, p.1

(11) Ibid, p.10.

(12)S.J. Duly, <u>The Resources of the Empire</u> (London : 1924), pp.33, 128.

(13)J & F Grover Ledger 1847-1855; L.M.A. ACC/0694/002.

(14)Ibid, p.28

(15)Ibid, p.341.

(16)Ibid, p.423.

(17)Ibid, p.441.

(18)J & F Grover Estimates Book, 27[th]June 1859-29[th]July 1868; L.M.A. ACC/0694/007.

Notes: Chapter 4 : The Grovers as Undertakers

(1) <u>Mason's Directory</u> (1853), pp.42-55.

(2) J & F Grover Ledger 1847-1855; L.M.A. ACC/0694/002, p.2.

(3) Edwin Chadwick, "Report on the Sanitary Conditions of the Labouring Population: A supplementary report on the results of a special inquiry into the practice of internment in towns". (London; 1843), p.47ff. Cited in C. Brooks, "Burying Tom Sayers: Heroism, Class and the Victorian Cemetery", <u>Victorian Society Annual</u>, (1989) p.4-20.

(4) <u>Middlesex County Times</u>

(5) G. D. H. Cole & R. Postgate, <u>The Common People</u> (London: Methueun & Co. Ltd, Fourth edition 1971), 1937.

(6) J & F Grover Ledger,1847-1855; L.M.A. ACC/0694/002, p.238.

(7) Ealing census, 1841, 1851, T.N.A.

(8) Richardson, <u>Death</u>, p.67.

(9) Geoffrey Best, <u>Mid-Victorian Britain 1851-1875</u> (London: Fontana, 1971, p.117.

(10) Reverend E. W. Relton scrapbook, 1850-1888, L.M.A. DRO/037/A/12.

(11) Reverend Relton's scrapbook, 1850-1888, L.M.A. DRO/037/A/12.

(12) McEwan, Ealing p.31

(13) Ibid, p.39

(14) Reverend Relton's scrapbook, 1859-1865 L.M.A. DRO/037/A/11/001.

(15) Ealing Vestry Minutes 1860-1874 21st March 1875.

(16) Ibid. 31st March 1874.

(17) J & F Grover Ledger, 1866-1875 L.M.A. ACC/0694/004, p.39.

(18) Pigots Directory (1822/3).

(19) Post Office London Directory (1852)

(20) Curl, James Stevens, The Victorian Celebration of Death (Newton Abbot, 1972), p.141.

(21) Ruth Richardson, "Why Was Death So Big in Victorian Britain" in Ralph Houlbrooke ed. Death, Ritual and Bereavement, p.115.

(22) Ibid. p.117.

(23) Richardson, Death, p.276.

Notes to Chapter 5: The Victorian Funeral and the Undertaking Business 1830-1900

(1) Walter, Funerals p.55.

(2) Bertram Puckle, Funeral Customs. Their Origin and Development (London: 1926), p.97.

(3) Pat Jalland, "Death, Grief and Mourning in the Upper Class Family 1860-1914" in Houlbrooke, Death, p.180.

(4) Ibid. p.180

(5) Catharine Arnold, Necropolis: London and Its Dead (London: 2007), p.209.

(6) Litten, "Journeys", p.175.

(7) Puckle, Funeral Customs, pp.97, 98.

Bibliography

Manuscript sources

London Metropolitan Archives:

Apprenticeship Indenture:

DRO/020/E/03/001. Joseph Taylor to Mark Anthony Low of Spitalfields, 3rd July 1814.

Business Records:

ACC 0694/001 J & F, Grover Cash Book, 1841-1847.

ACC 0694/002 J & F, Grover Ledger, 1847-1855.

ACC 0694/003 J & F, Grover Ledger, 1860-1866.

ACC 0694/004 J & F, Grover Ledger, 1866-1875.

ACC 694/7 J & F, Grover Ledger, 1859-1892.

ACC 694 J & F, Grover Ledger, 1847-1855, notes made by Mr Dallory on the business records.

Ealing Burial Register

DRO/037/A/01/033 May 1843-October 1857.

Ealing Census 1831:

ECH/KMH/5, Letter dated 19th November 1958 containing extracted statistical information on 1831 census from the County Archivist.

Ealing Parish Records:

Rural Deanery: Scrapbook of Reverend Relton and Newspaper cuttings:

DRO 037/A/12/004, 1864-1867

DRO 037/A/11/001, 1859-1865.

DRO 037/A/12/1, 1853-1881.

DRO 037/A/12/3/001, 1853-1881.

DRO 37/A/12/003/01, 1884-1888.

Ealing Overseers of the Poor:

ACC 2208/E/115, Note book their A.

ccounts, 1836-1837.

ACC 2208/E/123, Tenders for Contracts

ACC 2208/E/124, Register of Ealing Apprentices.

ACC 2208/E/125, List of Ealing's Paupers with notes.

Inventory:

DL/AM/PI/01/1719/003 Inventory of Thomas Phil Undertaker of St Martin's in the Field 11th February 1717.

Ealing Local History Library:

993/6 Middlesex County Times 15[th]April 1882

1517/4 Middlesex County Times 14th May 1892

Vestry Minutes 1860 1874, p.616

Guildhall Library:

Broadside 24.100. London c.1720.

London Museum:

As on Public display in 1990 / 1991. Advertisement for Dickens & Co., Furnishing Undertakers, near the Euston Road, London, c. 1860's.

The National Archives:

TNA HO 107/689 Census records relating to Ealing, 1841

TNA HO 107/1699 Census records relating to Ealing, 1851

Society of Genealogists' Library, London:

Indices to apprenticeship records in Public Record Office, 1710-62 and 1762-74.

Undertakers listed in connection with burials at Wesley's Chapel, City Road, London 1779-1854, mf.

PRINTED SOURCES:

Primary sources: Books and Directories:

Glen, William Cunningham, The Burial Board Act of England and Wales, with Introduction, Notes, Cases and Index. (London: 1858)

Hazlitt, W. Carew, The Livery Companies of the City of London 1892.

Holden's Triennial Directory, Vol. 1 (1808).

Kelly's Suburban Post Office Directory (1909)

Kelly's Commercial Directory, Vol. 2. (1920).

Kent's London Directory (1809).

Mason's Directory, Brentford and Ealing, (1853).

Post Office London Directory (1842).

Post Office London Directory (1846).

Post Office London Directory, Trades (1852).

Post Office London Directory, Trades & Court (1875).

Turner, J. Burial Fees for the Principal, Churches, Chapels and New Burial Grounds in London and it's Environs with list of searchers, hours of burial, early dues and all necessary information for undertakers. London: c.1838).

Universal British Directory of Trade, Commerce and Manufacture Vol. 1. (1797).

Walford, Edward Village London Vol. 1, (Cassell & Co., first published 1883, reprinted by Alderman Press 1983).

Secondary sources:

Arnold, Catharine, Necropolis: London and Its Dead (London: Simon & Schuster, Pocket edition 2007).

Best, Geoffrey, Mid-Victorian Britain 1851-1875 (London: Fontana, 12th edition 1990).

Blake, Margaret, Foklore and Customs of Rural England (Newton Abbot: David Charles PLC, Paperback edition 1988).

Brooks, Chris, "Burying Tom Sayers: Heroism, class and the Victorian cemetery". Victorian Society Annual (1989).

Cole, G.D.H. and Raymond Postgate, The Common People (London: Methuen & Co., 4th edition 1971).

Curl, James, S. The Victorian Celebration of Death (Newton Abbot, 1972).

Duly, S. J. ed. The Resources of the Empire (London: 1924).

Ealing Local History Society: <u>Local Historian</u>: 1961, no.1; 1961, no.2; 1962/1; 1962/2; 1962/3; 1963/1; 1963/2; 1963/3; 1964/1; 1964/ Part 2; 1965/2; 1966/2; 1966/1; 1967/1.

Goulty, George, A. "Nelson's Memorial Rings", <u>Genealogists' Magazine</u> Vol. 23 (1990).

Harrison, J.F.C., <u>Early Victorian Britain 1832-1851</u> (Glasgow: Fontana, 1979).

Harrison, J.F.C., <u>Late Victorian Britain 1875-1901</u> (Glasgow: Fontana, 1990).

Heal, Sir Ambrose, <u>Signboards of Old London Shops</u> (London: B.T. Batsford, 1947).

Houlbrooke, Ralph, <u>Death, Ritual and Bereavement</u> (London: Routledge & Kegan, 1989).

Jones, Barbara, <u>Design for Death</u> (London: Andre Deutsch Limited, 1967).

Laslett, Peter, <u>The World We Have Lost – further explored</u> (London: Methuen & Co. Ltd, 3rd edition 1983).

Litten, Julian, "Journeys into Paradise", <u>Genealogists' Magazine</u> Vol.23 (1990).

McEwan, Kate, <u>Ealing Walkabout</u> (Ealing: Pulse Publications, 1983).

May, Trevor, <u>The Victorian Undertaker</u> (Buckinghamshire: Shire Publications Ltd, 2007).

Meller, Hugh, <u>London Cemeteries: An Illustrated Guide and Gazetter</u> (Amersham: Avebury Publishing Co., 1981).

More, Charles, The Industrial Age: Economy and Society in Britain 1750-1985 (London: Longmans Inc. 1990).

Polson, C. J., Disposal of the Dead (London: English Universities Press Ltd, 2nd editon 1962).

Porter, Stephen, Exploring Urban History (B.T. Batsford Ltd. 1990).

Puckle, Bertram, Funeral Customs, Their Origin and Development (London: 1926).

Richardson, Ruth, Death, Dissection and the Destitute (London: Routledge & Kegan Paul, 1987).

Sanders, Peter, The Simple Annals (Gloucester: Alan Sutton, 1989).

Victoria County History Vo.7. (Oxford: Oxford University Press, 1982).

Walter, Tony, Funerals and How to Improve them (Kent: Hodder & Stoughton, 1990).

Whittledon, Eric, H., The Grover Family of Ealing (Ealing: Ealing Museum, Art and History Society, 1982).

Appendix 1

Business Transactions of J & F Grover 1847-1855

ATKINSON: 14 entries for sundries

ATLEE, Mr R.: 2 sundry entries

ATLEE, Mr R.: Funeral (p.664)

ATLEE, Miss: 2 sundry entries

ATLEE, Mrs Jno.: Funeral (p.494)

ATLEE, Mrs Stephen : Funeral (p.664)

AUSTIN: 1 sundry entry

BANNISTER, Esq.

BARFOOT, Mr: Making mattrass (mattress?)

BARFOOT, Esq. H.

BARFOOT, Mr: 3 sundry entries

BARLOW, Miss: inventory

BARLOW, Mrs: 5 sundry entries

BARLOW, Miss: closet in w/c

BARROW, Mrs: 8 sundry entries

BASS, Mr F.: Funeral (p.242)

BEAUCIIAMP, Mr: 2 sundry entries

BEAUCHAMP, Mr: Funeral (p.183)

BENNISON, Esq.

BIDDER, Mrs: 8 sundry entries

BIDWELL, Esq. J: 3 sundry entries

BIGGS, Mr.: Funeral (p.348)

BIGGS, Mr.: Funeral (p.537)

BINNEY, Esq.

BIRD, Mr: work at J. Percival Esq.

BLAGROVE, Mr J: new shutters

BLAKE, Mr

BOYS School Trustees: 3 repair entries

BRILL

BRILL, Mr: New notice board

BRINCE, Mr

BROOKS, Mr Funeral (p.288)

BROWN, Mr

BURTON, Miss: needlework cushion

BURTON, Miss: bedchair-padded and covering

BURTON, Miss: 5 sundry entries

BUSWELL / BOSWELL, Mr

BUTLIN, Esq Jno: 2 repair entries

BUTLIN, Esq Jno: 4 sundry entries

BUTLIN, Esq J: 2 repair entries

BUTLIN, Esq J: 20 sundry

BUTLIN, Exors. of: Funeral (p.446)

BYE, Way Trustees: 13 repair entries

CAVENDISH, Mrs

CHAMBERS, Mr: 4 sundry entries

CHAMBERS, Mr: new spout

CHARD, Mr R.: 3 Sundry entries

CHARD, A.: new boxes

CHARD, Mrs

CHOROU (?): Miss Ashton House

CHRISTCHURCH

CHURCHWARDENS: 9 sundry entries

CHURCHWARDENS: 1 repair

CLUTTON, Mr

CLUTTON, Miss

COLEMAN, Mr: Funeral (p.287)

COPE, Mr: Funeral (p.48)

COUNTY Fire Office: Mrs Nicholas

COWLEY, Mrs

CRAMP, Mrs

CRICKET Club: new boxes etc.

CRISP, Mr: Funeral (p.188)

CRISP: Funeral (p.238)

CROOKE: 2 sundry entries

CROSS, Mr Jos'h: Funeral (p.181)

CROSLEY, Mrs: 2 sundry entries

CURTEIS (CURTIS?) Esq.: 2 sundry entries

DARK: Funeral (p.451)

DEAN Common Committee: repairs

DENCE, Miss: Padded room

DENCE, Miss: 5 sundry entries

DOUGLAS, Mrs: 2 sundry entries

DUNLOP, Mrs: 5 sundry entries

DUNLOP, Mrs: Funeral (p.557)

EADEY, Mr: Funeral (p.295)

EDEN, Mr C.

EVANS, Esq. Geo.: 15 sundry entries

FARNELL: repairs at New Inn

FARNELL, Misses: repairs at New Inn

FARNELL, Misses: 2 sundry entries

FARNELL, Misses: repairs at Bell

FARQUHARSON, Mrs: Funeral (p.129)

FENN

FETTON: Funeral (p.21)

FISHER, Mr.: Funeral (p.241)

FRANKLIN, Mrs: Funeral (p.353) + 2 sundry entries

FOOT: Funeral (p.138)

FOUNTAIN, Mr.: 8 sundry entries

FOUNTAIN, Mr: Funeral (p.484)

FOUNTAIN, Mr: Funeral (p.264)

FOUNTAIN, Mr.: Funeral (p.572)

GARCIA, Esq.

GARDINER, Mrs

GARDINER, Mr.: Funeral (p.296)

GILBERT, Esq. G.: 7 sundry entries

GILES, Mr: 3 sundry entries

GILES: Funeral (p.587)

GILES, Mrs

GOODRICH, Mr

GOODRICH, Mrs: Funeral (p.672)

GOODRICH, Mr, M (N?): new table

GOODRICH, Mr R.: Funeral (p.281)

GOODRICH, Mrs: 6 sundry entries

GOODRICH, Mr R.: Funeral (p.144)

GRANT, Exors. of late: Funeral (p.168)

GREGORY, Mrs 2 sundry entries

GRIST, Mrs J. Exors. of: Funeral (p.132)

GRIST, Mrs: 4 sundry entries

GRIST

GROVER, Mr H.: 6 sundry entries

GROVER, Mr H.: Funeral (p.119)

GROVER, Mr H.: sawing

GROVER, Mr

GROVER, Mrs H.: abstract

HAMMOND, Mr

HAMMOND, Mr.: repair entry to cottages

HARBOUR, Mr

HARMAN, E.D. Esq. of Gerrards Cross: new table

HARRISON, Esq.: new table

HAY, Mrs

HAYLES,: 3 sundry entries

HAYWOOD, Mr H.: Langley Cottage

HEMMINGS

HENDERSON, Misses: 4 sundry entries

HENDERSON, Esq.: 3 sundry entries

HILL, Mrs

HOPGOOD, J. Esq.

HOPGOOD, Thos.: 5 entries

HUDSON: Funeral (p.396)

IBBOTSON, Miss: 2 sundry entries

ILSLEY (?), Mr J. Exors. of: Funeral (p.65)

IVES, Miss

IVES, Mrs J.: 2 sundry entries

IVES, Mrs

IVES, Mr Thos.: 5 sundry entries

IVES, Mr Jas.: 3 sundry entries

IRVING, Miss: Making up Ottoman

IRVING, J. Reverend: 9 sundry entries

IRVING, J. Reverend: Funeral (p.617)

JOHNSON, Esq.: 4 sundry entries

JOHNSON, Esq.: 1 repair entry

JOYCE, Mr

JUSTAMOND, (?) Mrs: 10 sundry entries

JUSTAMOND, (?) Mrs and Dr Tattersall

KIDSTON, Esq. : Funeral (p.18)

KING, Mr Jno.: Funeral (p.70)

KING, Mr Jno.: Funeral (p.71)

KING, Mr Jno.: Funeral (p.72)

KING, Mr Jno.: Funeral (p.76)

KING, Mr Jno.: Funeral (p.113)

KING, Mr Jno.: Funeral (p.114)

KNEVETT, Mrs: 2 sundry entries

LACEY, Mrs: 2 sundry entries

LAWFORD, Mr J.: 4 sundry entries

LAMBERT, Esq. S.: 3 sundry entries (236 Regent Street)

LAWRENCE, Mr: 8 sundry entries, including one making up tray at 54 Parliament Street

LAZENBY, Esq.: 13 sundry entries

LEES, Mr

LIGHTFOOT, Exors. of: Funeral (p.444)

LODDER, Mr: / sundry entries

MACEY, Mrs E.: Exors. of: Funeral (p.488)

MACLEOD, Mrs

MEACOCK, Jno.: Repairs at Minton Villas

MEACOCK, Jno.: 7 sundry entries

MERRICK, RICH. Esq.: 2 sundry entries

MERRICK, Mrs.: 2 sundry entries

MILLS, Mr G.

MITCHEL, Mr

MONTOGOMERY, Mr.: 3 sundry entries

MOORE, Mr

MORSE, E. Esq.: 9 sundry entries

MORSE, E. Esq.: new sash in w/c

MOSELEY, Esq.: 2 sundry entries

MURPHY, Mrs: 7 sundry entries, including one making blinds

NEIGHBOUR, Jno: Funeral (p.481)

NEWTON, Mr: 3 sundry entries

NICHOLAS, Dr.: 23 entries, including 2 at Wadham House

NICHOLLS, Esq.: 6 sundry entries

NORTHLEIGH, Miss: 2 sundry entries

NUNN, Miss

NYE, Mr

OAKELY, Mr: Funeral (p.44)

O'HARA, Mr: 3 sundry entries

OLDING, Mr: 2 sundry entries

PARRAMORE, Mrs

PARRY, Esq.: 3 sundry entries

PATTEN, Mrs

PEARSON, Exors. of: Funeral (p.538)

PERCEVAL, (?)Miss: (boxes and lights)

PERCEVAL, (?) Miss: 13 sundry entries

PERCEVAL, (?), Esq.: 10 sundry entries

PERCIVAL, (?) Miss

PICHOU (?), Esq.

POOLE, R. Esq.

PORTER, Mr H.

PORTER, Mr

POWELL, Mrs R. exors of: Funeral of (p.62)

PRICE, Mr Thos. Exors of: Funeral (p.665)

PRICE, Mr: Funeral (p.538)

PRICE, Mr

PUTNAM, Mr: Funeral (p.559)

RADCLIFFE, Mr: Funeral (p.175)

RAILTON, J. Esq.: repairs to stables

RAILTON, J. Esq.: 2 sundry entries

RAILTON, J. Esq.: abstract

RAY: 8 sundry entries

RAY AND GROVER: Messrs repair entry

RAY, Mr: repair entry

RAY, Mr: Funeral (p.599)

REDHEAD, Mr S.

RICHARDS, Mrs G.: repairs at Castle Bar

RICHARDS, Mrs G.: sundry entries

ROBINSON, Mrs

RODD, Esq. exors of: work at vault

RODD, Mrs: 7 sundry entries

ROSE, Mrs: Funeral (p.272)

ROSE, Mr: Funeral (p.287)

SCRIVEN, Esq. Jno.: repairs

SCRIVEN, Esq. Jno.: sundry entries

SCRIVEN, Esq. J.

SCRIVEN, Mr W. Exors. of: Funeral (p.286)

SELBY, Esq.: Funeral (p.609)

SEYMOUR, Esq. J.

SIDLEY, Edw.: Funeral (p.4)

SIMMONDS, Mr: New box

SLARK, E. Mr.: 2 sundry entries

SLARK, Mr R.: repairs at cottages

SLARK, Mr R.: 7 sundry entries

SLARKEY, Mrs

SLEVVY, Mr

SMALLMAN, Mrs: Funeral (p.441)

SMALLMAN, Mrs: 2 sundry entries

SMITH, Mrs: Funeral (p.576)

SMITH, Esq.: putting on door chains

SQUIRE, Mr: Packing etc.

STAMMERS, Mr: Funeral (p.595)

STARKEY, Mrs: 2 sundry entries

STARKEY, Chas. Exors. of: Funeral (p.2)

STEVENS, Mr: Packing

STEVVY, Mrs: 2 sundry entries

STEWARDS of Ball at Assembly Rooms

STONE, Mr: Funeral (p.240)

STRATFORD, Mrs: Funeral (p.520)

STRATFORD, Mr J.: new sashes at Mr. T. Edens

SWAN, Mrs: Funeral (p.360)

TAME, Mrs: Funeral (p.155)

TARGET, Mr: 2 sundry entries

TATTERSALL, Dr and Mr JUSTAMOND

TATTERSALL, Dr: oil cloth entry

TATTERSALL, Dr: 17 sundry entries

TATTERSALL, Dr: Funeral (p.615)

TATTERSALL, Dr.: Funeral (p.182)

TAYLOR, Mr G.: Funeral (p.405)

TAYLOR, Mrs G.: 6 sundry entries

TAYLOR, Mrs G.: Funeral (p.670)

THANE, Miss (Cecil Lodge)

THOMSON, Mr B.: 8 sundry entries

THOMSON, Mr: New boxes

THOMSON, Mr J.: 3 sundry entries

THOMSON, Mrs: 3 sundry entries including one at Gower House

THORN, Mr J.: 4 sundry entries

TIDY, Mr exors. of the late: Funeral (p.663)

TIDY, Mr W.: Funeral (p.90)

TOOLEY, Mr: Funeral (p.121)

TRYE, Mrs: 4 sundry entries

TRYE, Mrs: covering chair

VERNON, Mrs: work al 45 Burton St.

VERNON, Mrs: 3 sundry entries

VIVEASH, Chas esq.: 2 sundry entries

WAKELIN, Mr or WAHELEN

WALPOLE, Esq. S. H.: 3 sundry entries

WARNE, Mr

WARNER, Esq. Jno. Senior: Funeral (p.487)

WAUGH, Mrs (at Mrs Montgomerys)

WEATHERLEY, Esq. E.

WEBSTER, Esq. G.

WEBSTER, Esq. G.: 10 sundry entries

WELCH, Miss E.: repairing blinds

WELCH, Miss E.: 4 sundry entries

WELCH, Esq. senior, 13 Wyndham Place, Bryanstone Square

WELCH, Esq. senior: new blinds

WELCH, Esq. senior

WELLS, Mr

WELLS, Mr: Funeral (p.282)

WELLS, Mr: Funeral (p.59)

WEST, Mr: Funeral (p.663)

WHEELER, Mr

WHITE, Mr

WHITELY: Funeral (p.281)

WIDNALL, Mr

WILLES, Exors. of: Funeral p.(292)

WILLS, Mr Jno.

WILLS, Mr J.: 6 sundry entries

WILSON, Miss

WOLSELEY, Mrs Exors. of: Funeral (p.490)

WOOD, Esq. Geo. : 10 sundry entries

WOOD, Esq. Geo. : 8 sundry entries

WOD, Esq. G.: Funeral (p.510)

WOD, Miss: 6 sundry entries

WRIGHT, Mr J.: packing furniture

YATES, Mr: Funeral (p.127)

Appendix 2

Funerals Arranged by J & F Grover 1847-1855

Funerals in the Grover ledger were listed by the person arranging the funeral of the deceased, rather than under the deceased's name

ATLEE, Mr R.:

Mrs Sarah ATLEE, 73 years, 15th March 1853, Ealing - two pounds thirteen shillings. (p.664)

ATLEE, Mrs S.:

Mr Stephen ATLEE, 81 years, 20th March 1853, Ealing - three pounds nine shillings and six pence. (p.664)

ATLEE, Mrs Jno.:

Mr Jno. ATLEE, 19th Oct. 1851 Ealing - two pounds thirteen shillings. (p.494)

BASS, Mr F.:

An infant , 27th May 1849, no cemetery given - eight shillings. (p.242)

BEAUCHAMP, Mr:

Master W.R.R.SLADE, 26th October, no cemetery given. (p.183)

BIGGS, Mr:

Mrs A. BIGGS, 9th April 1850, no cemetery given two pounds nine shillings and three pence. (p.348)

BIGGS, Mr G.:

Mrs Mary PEARSON, 11TH January 1852 – two pounds ten shillings and five pence. (p.537)

BROOKS, Mr G. :

An infant, 23rd September 1849, no cemetery given – one pound fourteen shillings and nine pence. (p.288)

BUTLIN, John Esq.:

Exors of: Funeral, 2nd April 1851 Ealing sixty four pounds five shillings and six pence. (p.446)

COLEMAN, Mr H. M. :

John ROSE, 5th September 1849 Ealing – two pounds nine shillings and nine pence. (p.287)

COPE:

Phillip Robert COPE 8th August, 1857, no cemetery given – one pound fourteen shillings and nine pence. (p.48)

CRISP, Mr:

Use of Pall, Frances GROVER, 19th November, 1848, no cemetery given four shillings and six pence (p.188)

CRISP, Mr H.:

An infant, 22nd April 1849, no cemetery given - thirteen shillings. (p.238)

CROSS, Mrs Jo'sh.:

Josh CROSS, 19th October 1848, Ealing - ten pounds one shilling and three pence. (p.181) – Mrs Cross at Mrs Blakes.

DARK, Esq.:

Edward Robert DARK (youth), 18th April 1851, Ealing – six pounds five shillings and six pence (p.451)

DUNLOP, Esq.:

Andrew Robert DUNLOP, 36 years, 9th April 1852, Greenwich - thirty nine pounds six shillings. (p.557)

EADEY, Mr:

An infant, 10th October, 1849, no cemetery given. Thirty nine pounds six shillings. (p.557)

FARQUHARSON:

Mrs Ann FARQUHARSON, 16th April 1848, Ealing – two pounds sixteen shillings and six pence. (129) (The surveyors wife).

FETTON:

Mr William CANHAM, 23rd May 1847, Ealing – four pounds eight shillings and three pence. (p.21)

FISHER, Mr:

Mrs Adelaide FISHER, 13th May 1849, no cemetery given – two pounds. (p.241)

FOOT, Capt.:

Charlotte Elizabeth FOOT, 7th June 1848, Ealing - twenty nine pounds twelve shillings and six pence. (p.138)

FOUNTAIN, Mr:

Miss Annie Rebecca FOUNTAIN, a young woman, 27th June 1849, Ealing - five pounds seven shillings six pence (p.264) (The Draper's daughter).

FOUNTAIN, Mr:

Master Edwin Abraham FOUNTAIN of Ealing, an infant, 9 months, 11th July 1851. Ealing. Two pounds fourteen shillings and sixpence, (p.484)

FOUNTAIN, Mr:

Miss Ellen Maria FOUNTAIN, an infant 4 years, 10th June 1852, Ealing. Three pounds nineteen shillings and six pence.(p.572)

FRANKLIN, Mr:

Mrs Anne FRANKLIN, 22nd May 1850, Marylebone – nineteen pounds one shilling and eleven pence. (p.353)

GARDINER, Mr:

Mrs Mary GARDINER, 3rd November 1849, Ealing – six pounds nine shillings and three pence. (p.296)

GILES, Mrs:

Mr James Willaim GILES, a youth, 7th July 1852, Ealing - seven pounds fifteen shillings. (p.587)

GRIST, Mr Jas.:

Exors of Funeral: 27th April 1848, - twelve pounds eighteen shillings and six pence. (p132)

GOODRICH, Mr R.:

An infant, 5th July 1848, no cemetery given - nineteen shillings and six pence. (p.144)

GOODRICH, Mr R.:

An infant, 1st August, 1849, no cemetery given – six shillings and six pence. (p.281)

GOODRICH, Mrs:

Mr W'm GOODRICH, 36 years, 8th May, 1853, Ealing – six pounds nineteen shillings and six pence. (p.672)

GRANT, Mr S.:

Mrs S. GRANT, 15th August, 1848, Ealing – five pounds seventeen shillings and six pence. (p.168)

GROVER, Mr H.:

Miss Maria Elizabeth GROVER, 13th January, 1848, Ealing – six pounds two shillings. (p.119)

HUDSON, Mrs:

Wm. HUDSON, junior, 3rd November 1850, Ealing. Two pounds two shillings. (p.396)

ISLEY, Joel, Mr:

Exors of Funeral: 3rd October, 1847, Brentford – six pounds nineteen shillings and three pence. (p.65)

IRVING, Rev. J.:

Miss Caroline Earle IRVING, Ealing – eleven pounds six pence. (p.617)

KIDSTON, Esq.:

Mary Scott KIDSTON, 26th April, 1847, no cemetery given, coffin is taken to railway station – nine pounds eighteen shillings and six pence. (p.18)

KING, Mr Jno.:

Mr Thos. Wm BATTOCK, 7TH April 1847, Kensal Green – sixteen pounds thirteen shillings and eight pence. (p.70)

KING, Mr Jno.:

Mr Jno. KING, senior, 12th April 1847, Chapel, Brentford – ten pounds three shillings and four pence. (p.71)

KING, Mr Jno.:

Mr Jno. WALKER, 30th October 1847, Kensal Green – twelve pounds four shillings and five pence. (p.72)

KING, Mrs Jno.:

Mr Thos. SMITH BATTOCK, 3rd December 1847 Kensal Green – thirteen pounds fifteen shillings and four pence. (p.76)

KING, Mr Jno.:

Mrs Elizabeth Sarah SINCLAIR, 24th December 1847, Heston – ten pounds six shillings and seven pence (p.114)

KING, Mr Jno.:

Mr John SAUNDERS, 22nd December 1847, Hammersmith - ten pounds six shillings and seven pence. (p.114)

LIGHTFOOT, Matilda, Mrs:

Exors of: Funeral: 26th March 1851, Cowley forty one pounds twelve shillings and six pence. (p.444)

MACEY, Mrs E.:

Exors of: Funeral: 16th October 1851, Ealing – ten pounds three shillings. (p.488)

NEIGHBOUR, Mr W.:

Mr John NEIGHBOUR, 27TH July 1851, no cemetery given – two pounds five shillings and three pence. (p.481)

OAKLEY, Mr:

An infant, 1847, no cemetery given – eleven shillings. (p.44)

POWELL, Mrs Rebecca Ann:

Exors: Funeral: 1847, Ealing – thirty seven eleven shillings. (p.62)

PRICE, Mr:

Mrs Jane Price at Ealing Church, 23rd January 1852 – twenty nine pounds nineteen shillings. (p.538)

PRICE, Mr Thos.:

Exors: Funeral: 21st March 1853, Ealing – twenty eight pounds eighteen shillings. (p.665)

PUTNAM, Mr:

Mrs Anne LEAK, 9th May 1852, no cemetery given – two pounds six shillings. (p.559)

RADCLIFFE, Mr:

Miss Mary Jane RADCLIFFE, 24th September 1848 – two pounds three shillings and nine pence. (p.175)

RAY, Mr:

Mr George CARTER, 21 years, 15th August 1852 – four pounds nineteen shillings. (p.599)

ROSE, Mr:

Obediah ROSE, 21 years, 21st May 1849, cemetery – two pounds. (p.272)

ROSE, Mr:

Mr John ROSE, 11th September 1849, Ealing – one pound sixteen shillings and six pence. (p.287)

SCRIVEN, Mr Wm.:

Exors of: Funeral, 4th September 1849, Ealing – twenty two pounds one shilling and six pence. (p.286)

SELBY, Esq.:

Mrs Sarah Chisman SELBY, 17th September 1852, Birmingham – sixteen pounds fourteen shillings and six pence. (p.609)

SIDLEY, Edw.:

An infant, 21st February 1847, no cemetery given – eleven shillings and six pence. (p.4)

SLARK, Mrs Elizabeth:

25th November 1851, 76 years. (p.501)

SMALLMAN, Mrs Elizabeth:

Exors: Funeral: Late 5th Februrary 1851, Kensal Green – fifty eight pounds three pence. (p.441)

SMITH, Mrs:

Miss Helen SMITH, 14 years 8 months, 12th June 1852, Ealing – nine pounds eighteen shillings and six pounds. (p.576)

STAMMERS, Mr:

Mrs Susan STAMMERS: 3oth July 1850, Ealing – four pounds five shillings and three pence. (p.595)

STARKEY, Mr Chas.

Exors of: Funeral: 16th March 1847, Ealing – thirty one pounds eleven shillings and six pence. (p.2)

STONE, Mr:

An infant, 6th June 1849, no cemetery given eleven shillings and six pence. (P.240)

STRATFORD, Mrs:

Mr Wm. STRATFORD:, 4TH January 1852, no cemetery given – one pound fifteen shillings. (p.520)

SWAN, Mrs:

Master Geo. GROVENOR, 4th July 1850, no cemetery given – seventeen shillings. (p.360)

TAME, Mrs:

Mr Chas TAME: 2nd July 1848 – three pounds twelve shillings and six pounds. (p.155)

TATTERSALL, Dr:

Mrs Mary TATTERSALL, 9th November 1852, Ealing – thirty four pounds sixteen shillings and six pence. (p.615)

TAYLOR, Mr G.:

Selena BRYANT, 12th December 1850, no cemetery given – two pounds fifteen shillings. (p.405)

TAYLOR, Mr:

Jno. TAYLOR, 28 years, 24th April 1853, Check cemetery - two pounds two shillings. (p.670)

TIDY, Mr W.:

Mrs Mellier TIDY,: 23rd December 1847, no cemetery given – six pounds two shillings and six pence. (p.90)

TIDY, Mr W.:

Exors of: Funeral: 80 years, 28th February 1853, Ealing – four pounds eighteen shillings and six pence. (p.663)

TOOLEY, Mr:

Miss Sarah TOOLEY, 20th February 1848, Ealing – two pounds eleven shillings six pence. (p.121)

WARNER, Jno Esq:

Miss Frances WARNER, an infant, 3 years, 11th August 1851, Ealing churchyard – twenty pounds fifteen shillings and two pence. (p.487)

WELLS, Mr:

An infant, 29th August 1847, no cemetery given – thirteen shillings. (p.59)

WELLS, Mr:

Mrs Susan WELLS, 26th August 1849, Ealing – two pounds (p.282). (Mr Wells of Ealing Common)

WEST, Mr:

Mrs Sophy WEST, 60 years, 20th February 1853 – two pounds two shillings. (p.663)

WILLES, Mrs Margaret:

Exors: Funeral: 28th September 1849, Hillingdon – fifty nine pounds eighteen shillings and six pence. (p.292)

WHITLEY, Mr:

Edw'd J. WHITLEY, 10th August 1849, no cemetery given – three pounds two shillings and six pence. (p.281)

WOLSELEY, Mrs Eliza Anne (Ame?):

Exors: Funeral: 26th September 1851 Liverpool – forty seven pounds four shillings. (p.490)

WOOD, G. Esq.:

Mrs Ann ROSE, December 1851, no cemetery given. (p.510)

YATES, Mr:

Miss Sophia YATES, 26th March 1848, Ealing – six pounds eight shillings and six pence (p.127). (From Dr Nicholas).

Appendix 3

The People who were arranging funerals at J & F Grover's firm between 1847-1855

I have compared the names listed in the Grover ledger to the names listed in Mason's Directory and grouped them into the social group that they are listed under.

Abbreviations

G – Gentry in Mason's Directory

T – Traders in Mason's Directory

NR – no reference to in Mason's Directory

Unclassified – unable to group into a particular social class

ATKINSON - James ATKINSON Esq., Village Park (G)

ATLEE, Mr R. - Richard ATLEE, parish clerk and sexton, deputy register for the Brentford district, engine keeper, agent to the Albion Assurance Office (T)

ATLEE, Mrs Jno. - ATLEE surname only listed under Traders, likely to be member of the same family as above (T)

ATLEE, Mrs Stephen - As above

AUSTIN - (NR)

BANNISTER, Esq. – (NR)

BARFOOT, Esq. H - Henry BARFOOT Esq. Village Park (G)

BARLOW, Miss - Miss BARLOW, The Green (G)

BARLOW, Mrs - Probably the same as above, no BARLOWS listed under Traders in Mason's (G)

BASS, Mr - George BASS, Gardener and shopkeeper, near Old Church (T)

BEAUCHAMP, Mr - William BEAUCHAMP, grocer, The Green (T)

BENNISON, Esq. – (NR)

BIDDER, Mrs – (NR)

BIDWELL, Esq. J. – (NR)

BIGGS, Mrs George BIGGS, carpenter, Woodbine Cottage, Uxbridge Road (T)

BINNEY, Esq. – (NR)

BIRD, Mr - Miss Hamilton BIRD, professor of dancing, Melfort Villa (T)

BLAGROVE, Mr J. - Joseph BLAGROVE, Omnibus proprietor, Grove Cottage (T)

BLAKE, Mr - John BLAKE, marquee and rope maker, Uxbridge Road (T)

BRILL, Mr - Daniel BRILL, plumber, glazier, agent to the Union Assurance Office, Uxbridge Road (T)

BRINCE, Mr – (NR)

BROOKS, Mr - Francis BROOKES Esq 1 Circassian Place (G)

BROWN, Mr – (Unclassified)

BURTON, Miss – (NR)

BUSWELL / BOSWELL, Mr Charles BOSWELL, "Fox and Goose", Hanger Lane (T)

BUTLIN, Esq. Jno. - Mrs BUTLIN, Westfield House (G)

CAVENDISH, Mrs – (NR)

CHAMBERS, Mr – (Unclassified)

CHARD, Mr R. - Richard CHARD, boot and shoemaker, near the Old Church (T)

CHARD, A - Probably of the above family (T)

CHOROU, Miss – (NR)

CLUTTON, Mr – (NR)

CLUTTON, Miss – (NR)

COLEMAN, Mr - George James COLEMAN, Grocer and provision dealer, the Green (T)

COPE, Mr - Mr Henry COPE, boot and shoemaker, the Grove (T)

COWLEY, Mrs – (NR)

CRAMP, Mrs - Mrs Mary CRAMP, Lodging house keeper, the Green (T)

CRISP, Mr H. - Mr Henry CRISP, letter carrier, Church Lane (T)

CROOKE, - (NR)

CROSS, Mr Jos'h – (NR)

CROSLEY, Mrs - Mrs Ann CROSSLEY, 3 the Esplanade (G)

CURTEIS (CURTIS?) – (Unclassified)

DARK, Esq. - Frederick DARK "Feathers" (T)

DENCE, Miss – (NR)

DOUGLAS, Mrs – (NR)

DUNLOP, Mrs – (NR)

EADEY, Mr – (NR)

EDEN, R. C. - Charles EDEN, bread and biscuit maker (T)

EVANS, Esq. Geo. - George EVANS Esq. the Green (G)

FARNELL, Miss – (NR)

FARQUHARSON, Mrs - James FARQUHARSON, surveyor of the roads and sexton of Christchurch (T)

FENN - Meadow Cottage, Uxbridge Road (NR)

FETTON - (NR)

FISHER, Mr - (NR)

FRANKLIN, Mr - (NR)

FOOT, Capt. - (NR)

FOUNTAIN, Mr - Abraham FOUNTAIN, linen draper (T)

FRANKLIN, Mr - (NR)

GARCIA, Esq. F - Abraham GARCIA Esq. Sutherland House (G)

GARDINER, Mrs - (NR)

GARDINER, Mr - (NR)

GARDINER, Jnr. - (NR)

GILBER, ESQ. G. - (NR)

GILES, - Probably related to Margaret GILES (T)

GILES, Mrs - Margaret GILES, "New Inn" (T)

GOODRICH, Mrs - Lucy GOODRICH, baker opposite the Old Church (T)

GOODRICH, Mr - Probably related to the above (T)

GOODRICH, Mr M (N?) - Probably related to the above (T)

GOODRICH, Mr R. - Probably related to the above (T)

GRANT - (NR)

GREGORY, Mrs - Mrs GREGORY milliner, Thorn Place (T)

GRIST, Mr J. - Probably related to Mrs Elizabeth GRIST (G)

GRIST, Mrs - Mrs Elizabeth GRIST, Ealing Lane (G)

GROVER, Mr H. - Probably Humphrey GROVER, builder (1851 census) (T)

GROVER, Mr – (T)

HAMMOND, Mr - (NR)

HARBOUR, Mr - (NR)

HARMAN, E.D. Esq. – (NR)

Henry HARRISON Esq. Laburnham Cottage, Uxbridge Road (G)

HAY, Mrs - John HAY, Drayton Green (G)

HAYLES - Benjamin HAYLES, chemist and agent to the New Equitable Assurance Office, Uxbridge Road (T)

HAYWOOD, Mr H. - (NR)

HEMMINGS - Mr James HEMMINGS, the Green (G)

HENDERSON Misses - Andrew HENDERSON, Wadham Lodge (G)

HILL, Mrs - James HILL, furniture broker, Uxbridge Road or Thomas HILL, shopkeeper, 4 Grover Terrace, Guy's Lane (T)

HOPGOOD, J. - (NR)

HOPGOOD, Thos. - (NR)

HUDSON, Mrs - (NR)

IBBOTSON, Miss - (NR)

ILSLEY, Mr - (NR)

IVES, Miss - Probably related to Ives below (T)

IVES, Mrs - Mrs Maria IVES, schoolmistress, Ivy cottage (T)

IVES, Mr Thos. - Mr Thomas IVES, omnibus proprietor, Ivy cottage (T)

IVES, Mr Jas. - Probably related to the above (T)

IRVING, Miss - Probably related to Reverend IRVING (G)

IRVING, Reverend, J. - Not listed in the Directory, but Clergy usually Gentry class (G)

JOHNSON, esq. - Alfred Henry JOHNSON, farmer, Manor Farm, Gunnersbury (T)

JOYCE, Mr - James JOYCE Esq. Ealing Lane (G)

JUSTAMOND, Mrs - (NR)

KIDSTON, ESQ. - (NR)

KING, Mr Jno. - (NR)

KNEVETT, Mrs - Samuel KNEVETT, Esq. Ealing Lane (G)

LACEY, Mrs - (NR)

LAWFORD, Mr - John LAWFORD, bricklayer, Uxbridge Road (T)

LAMBERT, Esq. S. - Reverend William LAMBER, 2 Circassian Place, Guy's Lane (G)

LAWRENCE, Mr – (Unclassified)

LAZENBY, Esq. - William LAZENBY Esq. Woodland Place, Uxbridge Road (G)

LEES, Mr - (NR)

LIGHTFOOT - (NR)

LODDER, Mr - John LODDER "Rose and Crown" (T)

MACLEOD, Mrs – Mrs MACLEOD, 3 Alexander Terrace, Haven Green (G)

MEACOCK, Jno. - John MEACOCK, farmer, Little Ealing (T)

MERRICK, Rich. - (NR)

MERICK, Mrs - (NR)

MILLS, Mr G. - George MILLS, gardener, Uxbridge Road (T)

MITCHEL, Mr - James MITCHELL "Castle" (T)

MONTGOMERY, Mr - Thomas MONTGOMERY, Pitcher, tailor, Grosvenor House (T)

MOORE, Mr – (Unclassified)

MORSE, E. Esq. - Edward MORSE, Esq. Drayton Green (G)

MOSELEY, Esq. - Edward MOSELEY, Esq. Warden Villa, Uxbridge Road (G)

MURPHY, Mrs - Mrs MURPHY, Broomfield Place, Dean (G)

NEIGHBOUR, Jno. - Mrs Ann NEIGHBOUR, laundress, 4 the Grove Terrace, Guys Lane (T)

NEWTON, Mr - Thomas NEWTON senior and junior, wheelwright, Uxbridge Road (T)

NICHOLAS, Dr - Listed in both Gentry and Trades as Dr Francis NICHOLAS, DCL Ealing School, the Green (G)

NICHOLLS, Esq. - John B. NICHOLS Esq. Hanger Lane (G)

NORTHLEIGH, Miss - Prospect Villa (G)

NUNN, Miss - Edgar NUNN, 5 Western Villas (T)

NYE, Mr - Thomas NYE, builder, undertaker, the Green (T)

OAKELY, Mr - Mary OAKLEY, Prospect Place, Uxbridge Road (G)

O'HARA, Mr - (NR)

OLDING, Mr - (NR)

PARRAMORE, Mrs (NR)

PARRY, Esq. (NR)

PATTEN, Mrs - (NR)

PEARSON, Mr - Mr John PEARSON, Rose Cottage, Uxbridge Road (G)

PEARSON, Miss - Probably related to the above (G)

PERCEVAL, Miss - Misses PERCEVAL Manor House, the Green (G)

PERCIVAL, Esq. - Spencer PERCEVAL Esq. Elm Grove (G)

PERCIVAL, Miss, related to the above (likely to be a spelling error in the ledger) (G)

PICHOU, Miss - (NR)

POOLE, R. Esq. - (NR)

PORTER, Mr H. - Henry PORTER, boot and shoe maker, the Green (T)

POWELL, Mrs R. Mansell POWELL, Carpenter (T)

PRICE, Mr Thos. - related to Mr James Price Esq. (G)

PRICE, Mr - James PRICE Esq. 2 Ealing Terrace (G)

PUTNAM, Mr - (NR)

RADCLIFFE, Mr - (NR)

RAILTON, J. Esq. - (NR)

RAY, Mr - Willian Henry RAY, Academy, Thorn House (T)

REDHEAD, Mr S. - (NR)

RICHARDS, Mrs - Mrs Jane RICHARDS dressmaker, 2 Providence Place, Uxbridge Road (T)

ROBINSON, Mrs – (Unclassified)

RODD, Esq. - probably related to Mrs Rodd as below (G)

RODD, Mrs - Mrs RODD, South Lodge, the Green (G)

ROSE, Mrs - Mrs ROSE, Haven Green (G)

ROSE, Mr   Probably related to the above Mrs ROSE (G)

SCRIVEN, Esq. Jno - (NR)

SCRIVEN, Mr W. - (NR)

SELBY, Esq. - (NR)

SEYMOUR, Esq. J. - (NR)

SIDLEY, Edward - (NR)

SIMMONDS, Mr - John SIMMONDS, dairyman Broomfield dairy, Uxbridge Road (T)

SLARK, E. Mr - James SLARK Esq. Grove House, Ealing Grove (G)

SLARK, Mr R. - Probably related to the above (G)

SLARKEY, Mrs - (NR)

SLEVVY, Mrs - (NR)

SMALLMAN, Mrs - (NR)

SMITH, Esq. - Probably Charles Henry SMITH, Westernlebar (?) Cottage (G)

SQUIRE, Mr - (NR)

STAMMERS, Mr - William STAMMERS carpenter, 1 Providence Place, Uxbridge Road (T)

STARKEY, Mrs - Mrs Ann STARKEY, Church Lane (G)

STARKEY, Chas - Probably related to the above (G)

STRATFORD, Mrs - (NR)

STEVENS, Mr - either Robert STEVENS, market gardener, Uxbridge, or John STEVENS, grocer and cheesemonger, Uxbridge Road (T)

STEVVY, Mrs - (NR)

STONE, Mr - (NR)

STRUDWICK, Mr J. - James STRUDWICK Esq. Park Place (G)

SWAN, Mrs - (NR)

TARGET, Mr - William TARGET, furnishing undertaker 2 Hawthorn Villas (T)

TATTERSALL, Dr - Dr James TATTERSALL MD, the Green (G)

TAYLOR, Mr - T George TAYLOR, dairyman (G)

TAYLOR, Mrs - T probably related to the above (G)

TAME, Mrs - (NR)

THANE, Miss - Miss THANE, the Green (G)

THOMSON, Mr - possibly related to the below (T)

THOMSON, J. - John THOMPSON, market gardener (T)

THOMSON, Mrs - Mrs Janet THOMPSON, straw hat maker, near the Old Church (T)

THORN, Mr J. - (NR)

TIDY, Mr - (NR)

TIDY, W. (NR)

TOOLEY, Mr - (NR)

TRYE, Mrs - Mrs Ann TRYE, Great Ealing (G)

VERNON, Mrs - Mrs VERNON, the Green (G)

VIVEASH, Chas. - Chas Baskerville VIVEASH, Esq. 2 Maquarie place, Uxbridge Road (G)

WAKELIN, Mr – (Unclassified)

WALPOLE, Esq. S. H. - Right Hon. Spencer Horatio WALPOLE, M.P. the Green (G)

WARNE, Mr. - (NR)

WARNER, Esq. Jno. - (NR)

WAUGH, Mrs - (NR)

WEATHERLEY, Esq. E. - Edward WEATHERLEY Esq. 2 Singapore Villas, Uxbridge Road (G)

WEBSTER, Esq. E. - North Lodge, the Green (G)

WEBSTER, Esq. G. - Probably related to the above (G)

WELCH, Miss E. - (NR)

WELCH, Esq. Senr. - (NR)

WELLS, Mr – (Unclassified)

WEST, Mr - Thomas WEST coal dealer, Uxbridge Road (T)

WHEELER, Mr - (NR)

WHITE, Mr – (Unclassified)

WHITLEY, Mr - Samuel WHITLEY, boot and shoe maker or Thomas WHITLEY, shoe maker and beadle at the Old Church. (T)

WIDNALL, Mr - (NR)

WILLES, Mrs Margaret - (NR)

WILLS, Mr Jno. – (Unclassified)

WILLS, Mr J. – (Unclassified)

WILSON, Miss – (Unclassified)

WOLSELEY, Mrs -(NR)

WOOD, Esq. Geo. - George WOOD, Esq. Magistrate, Hanger Hill (G)

WOOD, Miss - Miss WOOD, the Elms, Hanger Hill (G)

WOOD, Esq. Thos. - Probably related to the above (G)

WRIGHT, Mr J. – (Unclassified)

YATES, Mr – (Unclassified)

Illustrations

Illustration on front cover: The Grover Family outside Wisteria Cottage, Ealing circ. 1890. From information with the photograph made at a later date by a member of the Grover family: Left to right, Frank Charles Grover bn.1862 ; Eliza Martha Grover bn. 1832, d. 1895 (widow) ; Francis Grover d. 1882 ; William Grover bn. 1868 ; Jessica Annie Grover bn. 1860 ; Ada Florence Grover bn.1865.   ©Ealing Local History Centre. The Borough Archive T307/271/15.

Illustration 1: Undertaker Shop Signs c. 1680-c.1740 (from Sir Ambrose Heal's Signboards of Old London Shops, pp.174, 175). (a) William Boyce, at Ye WHIGHT HART & COFFIN, in ye Grate Ould Bayley, Near Newgeat. C.1680. (b) William Grinley, at Ye sign of ye NAKED BOY & COFFIN, at ye Lower Corner of Fleet Lane. c. 1730. (c) ISSAC WHITCHURCH, removed from Fleet Lane to the THREE COFFINS, by the Ditch side, near Holborn Bridge. C. 1740.

Illustration 2: Thorn Place.   From information with the photograph made at a later date "Notice how the doorway has been embellished in comparison with the other houses as John Grover was a builder". Ealing Local History Centre. ©The Borough Archive L5826 78/79.

Illustration 3: Photograph of The New Inn Public House May, 2017 by ©Eileen Sanderson

Illustration 4: Wisteria Cottage, Ealing. Ealing Local History Centre. ©The Borough Archive.

Illustration 5: Employees of J. & F. Grover in the yard at Wisteria Cottage, Ealing. ©Ealing Local History Centre. The Borough Archive T307/271/16.

Illustration 6: Postcard of St Mary's Road, Ealing, Postcard of Ealing (undated late nineteenth century / early twentieth century).

Illustration 7: Postcard of St. Mary's Old Church, Ealing c. 1906.

Illustration 8: St Mary's Church today, South Ealing, London W5 by ©Eileen Sanderson.

Illustration 9: Trade Card of the Grover family business, Ealing. ©L.M.A. ACC/0694/008.

Illustration 10: Lychgate at St Mary's Church, South Ealing, London W5 by ©Eileen Sanderson.

Illustration 11: Photograph of South Ealing Cemetery, South Ealing Road, London W5 by ©Eileen Sanderson.

Illustration 12: Inscription: Reverend Relton on the Lychgate at St Mary's Church, South Ealing, London W5 by ©Eileen Sanderson

Table 1: The Grover Family of Ealing – showing how the trade of undertaking was the main occupation for several generations.   Information for this table primarily from: Whittledon, Eric, H., <u>The Grover Family of Ealing</u> (Ealing: Ealing Museum, Art and History Society, 1982).

Eileen Sanderson has a degree in History and an MA in Information Services Management. She is an ex Metropolitan Police Officer and has also worked for Birkbeck College, the Centre for Metropolitan History at the Institute of Historical Research, the BBC and the Women's Library. She has also worked in the funeral business. This booklet was partly based around a Diploma she completed in History of the Family and Genealogy in 1991.